WILLIAM E. MASIH
DISCERNING SPIRITS

Copyright © 2022 William E. Masih

Typesetting by Fresh Wind Publishing
www.freshwindpublishing.co.uk

The right of William E. Masih to be identified as the author of this work has been asserted by the organization in accordance with the Copyright, Designs and Patents Act 1988.

All rights reserved. No part of this production may be reproduced, stored in a retrieval system, or transmitted in any form or by any means, electronic, mechanical, photocopying, recording or otherwise, without the prior permission of the publisher or a licence permitting restricted copying.

Scripture quotations taken from The Holy Bible, New International Version® NIV® Copyright © 1973 1978 1984 2011 by Biblica, Inc. TM Used by permission. All rights reserved worldwide.

ISBN: 978-1-9163180-2-1

Cover design by Esther Kotecha
www.ekdesigns.co.uk

Printed in the UK

ENDORSEMENTS

'I have read your book which exposes the powers of darkness and affirms the need for the gift of discernment of spirits. It is written well and will be a great help to people oppressed by the demonic. We do not believe in demon possession. A person can have multiple evil spirits, but God does not allow the devil to be totally in charge of a person or they would be doomed! So, we talk about demonization rather than demon possession. Very good.'

Jill Southern
Executive Leader of Ellel Ministries International and Regional Director of A.E. Asia and China

'William Masih has a real burden to see the Gifts and the Power of the Holy Spirit released in full measure across the Body of Christ. William is clearly gifted by the Lord in the area of Deliverance and with "Discerning of Spirits". His passion in to see believers moving in the Gifts, especially "The Discerning of Spirits.'

Pastor Ian Christensen
Senior Pastor of New Life Christian Centre Int'l

DEDICATION

This book is lovingly dedicated to my lovely wife
Darkhshinda William and to our children
Naysa William, Remelia William, Nathania William
and to all of our Church Family.

CONTENTS

Introduction..9

1. The Gifts of the Holy Spirit....................................13
   I. Categories of the gifts.......................................16
2. The Discerning of Spirits......................................18
   I. What the Discerning of Spirits is.....................20
   II. What the Discerning of Spirits is not..............20
   III. What the Discerning of Spirits does..............21
3. The Spirit of Rebellion (Herodias)........................23
4. The Spirit of Servanthood and Compassion (Phoebe)....32
5. The Spirit of Backsliding (Lot)..............................37
6. The Spirit of Faithfulness (Bezalel).......................48
7. The Spirit of Disbelief and Religion (Esau)..........56
8. The Spirit of Perfect Obedience and Submission (Mary)....65
9. The Spirit of Deception (Judas Iscariot)...............75
10. The Spirit of True Happiness and Joy (Noah)....85
11. The Spirit of Worldly Desires (Lot's wife)..........98
12. The Spirit of Absalom.......................................107
13. The Spirit of Jezebel...115
14. The Spirit of Python...121
15. The Spirit of Leviathan.....................................126

INTRODUCTION

1 John 4:1
"Dear friends, do not believe every spirit but test the spirits to see whether they are from God..."

Discernment can show us both our weaknesses and God's strength.

As we are open and honest before God, discernment reveals the real "us". Nothing is hidden. He sees and knows everything about us.

Sometimes, we rely on our own words rather than God's power.

The multitude of false teachers, fake pastors, false prophets, and fake sign and wonder doers have surrounded us. It is essential to know the truth.

These days, everyone in the church wants the gift of performing miracles, healing and prophecy, but they do not want the gift of discerning spirits.

As good and evil have mixed very well. It is tough to know what is right and what is wrong. That's why now we need more the gift of discernment than ever before.

Discernment needs to be combined with a pure heart and the word of God. The discernment helps us become familiar with God's ways so we will not become vulnerable to the deception and false teachings, which can be wolves in sheep's clothing. (Matthew 7:15)

There is only one Devil or one Satan, but there are many evil spirits. They all have a particular type of personality and a specific way in which they like to operate.

The demons have two different names. They have their created name given to them by God when they were made. They also have a functional name, which will tell you what kind of spirit you are with dealing.

For example, some of the functional names of the demons are the spirit of lust, the spirit of anger, the spirit of murder, the spirit of competition, the spirit of rebellion, the spirit of manipulation, etc.

The spirits have different functions. In the New Testament, we see some can make people mute or blind (Mark 3:20-30), others can cause the possessed person to harm themselves (Mark 5:1-20).

There are many spirits in the world, good and evil. Some of them you deal daily and some of them you would be completely unaware of. The spirits in this world are not all good, some of them are evil. We all know that we need to be able to discern, by the power of the Holy Spirit, which one of them is good and which one is evil.

Often, people are used by the enemy, in the way they live, behave, and create discomfort, chaos and turmoil in other people's lives. They never realise that they are a tool in the hands of the enemy.

INTRODUCTION

We need to be aware of the attacks and the activities of the enemy. We need to know how the enemy works. Satan always works behind the scenes.

People know you by your words. Your words become your actions. Your actions become your character and your character becomes your personality.

Your spirit listens to what you speak daily. Spirits are attached to the words we speak. Do you know that?

When we speak the word of God, then we attract the Holy Spirit. Then the Holy Spirit works according to our words.

In the same way, demons are also listening to our words and our words give them authority and permission to work because there is power in our words and the enemy always used our words as source of authority.

Remember, Satan and his demons have no authority or permission to work in our lives. We give them authority, power, control, and permission by our words and by living a lifestyle of sinning.

If we do not have the spirit of discernment, then we cannot stand against the attacks of the enemy. The spirit of discernment helps us to avoid costly mistakes and gives us the ability to be prudent and to know and recognise whether truly these words or actions are from God or not.

I am writing this book to encourage you to take this miracle path; God is opening before you.

I pray that your heart and mind will open to a revelatory understanding of the discerning spirits. Please allow this book to help you open your spiritual eyes and see in the spiritual realm.

I want to say a big thank you to everyone who has contributed in any way for this book, especially Sajjad Ahmed and Anish Matthew.

My prayer for you as you read this book is that you will be filled with the power of the Holy Spirit and gain a more profound revelation of discerning spirits.

CHAPTER 1
GIFTS OF THE HOLY SPIRIT

1 Corinthians 12:4-11
There are different kinds of gifts, but the same Spirit distributes them. There are different kinds of service, but the same Lord. There are different kinds of working, but in all of them and in everyone it is the same God at work. Now to each one the manifestation of the Spirit is given for the common good. To one there is given through the Spirit a message of wisdom, to another a message of knowledge by means of the same Spirit, to another faith by the same Spirit, to another gifts of healing by that one Spirit, to another miraculous powers, to another prophecy, to another distinguishing between spirits, to another speaking in different kinds of tongues, and to still another the interpretation of tongues. All these are the work of one and the same Spirit and he distributes them to each one, just as he determines.

These are the gifts God has given to the church. No one can earn these gifts. These gifts are not optional to pick and choose as you wish, but if you do not wish to, you can deprive yourself from having it.

The Holy Spirit gives these gifts. There are nine gifts of the Holy Spirit. All these nine gifts of the Holy Spirit are different from each other. Still, they are so linked and interlinked by the Holy Spirit that sometimes it is difficult to determine exactly which gift is in manifestation.

The following are a brief definition of each gift of the Holy Spirit.

THE WORD OF WISDOM
A word of God's wisdom is just that: a word. It is the revealing of the prophetic future under the anointing of God.

THE WORD OF KNOWLEDGE
It is the revealing of a fact in existence that can only be supernaturally revealed. It cannot be seen or heard or known naturally.

THE DISCERNING OF SPIRITS
It has to do with the comprehending of the human Spirit, supernaturally revealed by the Holy Spirit, good and bad. With this gift, you can look straight through a person and know whether he is telling the truth. (This book delves mainly about this gift)

THE GIFT OF FAITH
In the gift of faith, God brings to pass a supernatural change. No human effort is involved.

THE GIFT OF WORKING OF MIRACLES
The gift of the working of miracles does work through a human instrument. It is a person doing a supernatural act by the divine energy of the Holy Spirit.

THE GIFTS OF HEALING
In the gifts of healing, God supernaturally heals the sick through a ministry anointed by the Holy Spirit.

A person is given a gift from God's Spirit to pray for healing from a particular kind of sickness or disease. There might be as many gifts as there are diseases. That is why the term is in the plural form.

THE GIFTS OF TONGUES
The gift of tongues is a gift from the Spirit, to pray and proclaim a message from God in a language not understood by the person speaking it. This is because he has not studied that language and does not know it. He does not speak it from his mind but his Spirit.

THE INTERPRETATION OF TONGUES
When a message in tongues has been given, then the gift of the tongues' interpretation goes into operation. The message that has been given in tongues is interpreted supernaturally by the Holy Spirit through another person, without the person's mental capabilities being involved.

THE GIFT OF PROPHECY
The prophecy gift is the anointed speaking forth of words of edification, exhortation and comfort words supernaturally

given to a person or group of people from God.

I. CATEGORIES OF THE GIFTS

The spiritual gifts are like a chain, each one is linked to the other, so that when you pull one, you are pulling the entire chain. Sometimes it is not easy to separate the links and distinguish between them because they are so interrelated.

All these nine gifts of the Holy Spirit are divided naturally and spiritually into three categories:

1. Revelation Gifts
2. Power Gifts
3. Inspiration Gifts

THE REVELATION GIFT
Within this category, there is the Word of wisdom, the Word of knowledge and the discerning of spirits.

THE POWER GIFTS
This category of power gifts includes the gift of faith, the gift of healing and miracles.

THE INSPIRATION GIFTS
This category includes the gift of prophecy, the gift of speaking in tongues and tongues' interpretation.

THE DISCERNING OF SPIRITS
Before I say anything about this gift, we need to know what

the discerning of spirits is not because there are so many misunderstandings about this gift.

CHAPTER 2
THE DISCERNING OF SPIRITS

SEXUAL EVIL SPIRITS

There were two girls who were possessed by sexual evil spirits. They were living in different locations and God delivered them very powerfully.

One girl named Julia (name changed to protect identity) used to come to our church and was oppressed by a sexual evil spirit. She went to see her cousin in the village, and something happened over there. She was under the control of a sexual evil spirit when she came back. She told her mother that her cousin had sex with her, but her cousin denied it. When she came back to Islamabad, she started blaming other people that they had sex with her. Her father was outraged and wanted to fight with these people. He desperately wanted to report to the police.

But one day, Julia blamed her father as well and she told her mother what her father had done to her. She was in this condition for several months and every day she used to describe a new story. Her parents were nominal Christian and were not bold enough to discuss their daughter's problem with anyone else. They took her to different witch doctors. Most of them had beaten her very severely. (Most witch doctors in Pakistan usually inflict physical pain to cure the possessed.)

One day her mother narrated Julia's ordeal to one of the ladies who attends our church. She approached me and mentioned about Julia's situation.

I knew that there are two sexual evil spirits, Incubus and Succubus (male and female), so I told Julia's parents that they do not need to worry, she will be alright. When we went to their house as a team, this girl was in a terrible situation. Julia had bruises all over her face and body. We ministered to this girl and commanded this sexual evil spirit to leave her in Jesus' mighty name and immediately God set her free. Now she is married and happily living with her family.

SPIRIT OF BLASPHEMY

A lady named Jenny (name changed), who was not our church member, was possessed. She was married and had three children. She was living near one of our affiliated churches and she had two spirits – a sexual evil spirit and a blasphemy spirit.

Her husband was distraught because of her behaviour and the stories she was telling him. Jenny used to blame her father-in-law and one of her brothers-in-law that they were having sex with her at night as she was living in a joint family system. Sometimes she used to say that Jesus had sex with her, and she used to swear at Jesus. She always used to speak blasphemous words on Jesus, and she hated Jesus. Somebody told her husband about our church and when they came to our church, we prayed. We commanded the spirits of blasphemy and sexual evil spirits to leave Jenny and God delivered her immediately. Later she took water baptism and since then she has been coming to our church and became a part of the worship team. Praise God.

I. WHAT THE DISCERNING OF SPIRITS IS

The discerning of spirits is the divine ability to see the presence and activity of a spirit that motivates a human being, whether good or bad. The discerning of spirits is a gift that gives the believer power to see what others do not see. The discerning of spirits is a gift of the Holy Spirit that makes the possessor see into the Spirit world. By this insight, someone can discern God's similitude, the risen Christ, the Holy Spirit, Cherubim and Seraphim, the archangels and the host of angels, or Satan and his legions.

There are three areas in which these gifts can operate:
- The divine
- The demonic
- The human or natural

II. WHAT THE DISCERNING OF SPIRITS IS NOT

The discerning of spirits has no relationship to that which is natural. It is not some metaphysical operation. It is not mind reading. It has nothing to do with the realm of the mind. Some people claim to have "the gift of discernment." It is not a discernment of things; it is the discernment of spirits.

III. WHAT THE DISCERNING OF SPIRITS DOES

The discerning of spirits gives members of the body of Christ insight into the Spirit world, a realm that their five physical senses - Touch, Sound, Sight, Smell and Taste cannot enter naturally or physically by ourselves. Sometimes, God uses our physical senses to reveal hidden spiritual secrets supernaturally. My two physical senses are very active, like smell and sight. Sometimes I get a nasty smell or see great darkness around me and then I know that God wants to show me more profound things which I cannot see with my natural eyes.

The gift of discerning of spirits starts to penetrate to the dividing of soul and spirit within a person.

This discerning of spirits can bring tremendous inspiration to a church body.

It can produce a real spirit of security against false doctrines, lies and all kinds of things that are fallacious.

It can enable a church to choose the proper men and women to fulfil their church's ministries.

The gift of discerning of spirits is an excellent instrument to clean out our churches. Many pastors and church leaders today are engaged in activities that are dishonest, false, and not right. Church members are living in sin, doing things opposed to the will of God for their lives.

Through the discerning of spirits, we can have a holy church without spot or wrinkle. (Ephesians 5:27)

CHAPTER 3
THE SPIRIT OF REBELLION (HERODIAS)

I was born into a Roman Catholic family in Punjab, Pakistan. I gave my life to Jesus when I was 17 years old and since that time, I have been walking with Jesus. My childhood was mediocre. It was not very good, and I was not a remarkably well-behaved student. I spent most of my time outside with my friends, wandering around the streets. All my friends were drug addicts and one of my friends died due to heavy drugs use. I was in a gang, and we use to fight rival gangs. Although as a gang member, I did not approve of all that they were doing, I had a deep hunger for God, and I wanted to know the true living God but did not know how to know Him and follow Him. So, my life was miserable, and I was not content at all. I had no peace and did not see the purpose of my life. I used to tell myself that I will die one day without achieving anything in life. For me, my life was meaningless. I used to think that maybe one day I will also start taking drugs and die an addict. I am very thankful to God that he picked me from that dirty pit. If Jesus did not choose me from there, maybe now, I might have been a drug addict, taking drugs with my friends, in some corner of Islamabad, or perhaps in jail with the gang, with whom I was an active member of. When I finished high school, I studied different religions like Hinduism, Sikhism, Baha'ism, New Age, Mormonism, Jehovah's Witness, Islam, and Buddhism. I did not learn all these religions at home, but I would actively go to their place of worship: studying Islam I visited the mosque; for Hinduism, it was a visit to the Hindu Temple; for Sikhism a visit to the Sikh temple and Baha'ism I would go to the Baha Centre. My overall conclusion, i.e., my exhaustive research and visits, was that God did not exist. When I went to college, I met a Christian friend who tried to evangelize me and I told him my overall conclusion:

"There is no God!"

He was persistent and added, "No, there is one true living God. All the other religions teach you how you can reach out to God, but only Christianity tells you how God can reach you." Each time we met, he reiterated: "There is a true living God, and you can see Him. Our God is not like other gods of this world. If you want to see Him, He will come and will talk to you."

So I told him, "If I can see Him or observe Him, He is not God."

He was relentless. Each time we met, he echoed that the God of Christianity can reveal himself in Christ. One day, I said to him that I wanted to challenge His God; whoever He is, I wanted to see him. I concluded, "Your God has 30 days. Within 30 days, I want to see Him." Delighted and confident, he affirmed that surely His God would come and talk to me during that time. He told me that every night before I go to bed I should pray. He told me to be very sincere and pray the following from my heart: "God, the creator of this universe, a true living God, whoever you are, come and show me your face I want to see you."

He then confirmed confidently, "He will come and will talk to you."

My response was, "That is so easy; I will do it!" So, I prayed for 29 nights, and nobody came. I used to tell my friends, "See, there is no God." However, something happened! On the 30th night, when I was sleeping, I heard a voice from outside. "William! William!"

Someone was calling my name. I went out to the kitchen side of the courtyard, but nobody was present. I was afraid and came back and slept again. After some time, I heard that same voice which was calling me:

"William! William!"

I ran outside, but there was no one present. I returned to my bedroom. While standing in the kitchen door, words came into my mind, and at that time, I did not know that these words were in the Bible. I responded,

"Here I am God, what do you want to show or tell me?" I saw a man in a white robe that came to the roof as I said those words. (In my country, roofs are flat and not sloping as they are in Europe.) The man walked down the stairs and stood in front of me and asked me,

"Will you allow me to come into your bedroom?"

I did not say anything. I just walked back to my bedroom and sat near the headboard of the bed. He came in and sat at the footboard of the bed. While He was sitting on the bed, he told me that He was Jesus. I did not believe Him. I said to the man:

"Okay, if you are Jesus, then my brother and sister-in-law are sleeping in that room (pointing towards their door). Go and bring them here."

The man went and brought my brother and sister-in-law into the room. I was still sitting at the same place. My brother and sister-in-law came, and they sat on the other side of the bed and the man who said that he was Jesus sat at the same place as before. Then all four of us prayed together. After praying, my brother and sister-in-law went back to their room, after some time, the man later left.

The next morning, my sister-in-law came to me and enquired if I had had a nightmare the previous night. I replied that I did not. She told me that she and her husband came to my room and witnessed me praying and crying.

I asked her, "Did you pray with me?" She responded, "No."

Then I asked her, "Did you see someone else in my room?"

"No," she replied, "You were alone praying and crying." When I testified to her that Jesus visited me, and I saw Jesus, she said that they could feel the presence of God in my room. That was the day when my life changed completely. After that day, I threw away all the books I had of different religions and since that day, Jesus is my Lord and Saviour. Now, the Bible is the only book I love and read.

Since that day, I have experienced many highs and lows in my life, but Jesus has never left me alone. He is forever with me in all kinds of circumstances because He has promised,

THE SPIRIT OF REBELLION (HERODIAS)

"I will never leave you nor forsake you." He is always with me.

Matthew 14:3-11
Herod had arrested John and bound him and put him in prison because of Herodias, his brother Philip's wife, for John had been saying to him: "It is not lawful for you to have her." Herod wanted to kill John, but he was afraid of the people because they considered John a prophet. On Herod's birthday, Herodias' daughter danced for the guests and pleased Herod so much that he promised with an oath to give her whatever she asked. Prompted by her mother, she said, "Give me here on a platter the head of John the Baptist." The king was distressed, but he ordered that her request be granted and had John beheaded in prison because of his oaths and his dinner guests. His head was brought in on a platter and given to the girl, who carried it to her mother.

Herodias had the spirit of Jezebel, who killed John the Baptist. John had the spirit of Elijah. The spirit of Jezebel attacked again on the spirit of Elijah. This time, she was successful as she had failed the first time.

Herod had the spirit of Ahab, who did not stop Jezebel from her evil plans. Jezebel used Ahab's power and authority to fulfil all her evil plans. In the same way, we see here that Herodias used Herod to fulfil all her evil desires. She got everything that she wanted.

By killing John the Baptist, Herodias fulfilled her plan and got what she wanted. Jezebel wanted to kill Elijah to cease the voice of the Lord, but she failed. In the same way,

Herodias attacked John the Baptist to end the voice of the Lord and this time she was succeeded.

In these days, this spirit is working very powerfully in the churches and trying to stop the voice of the Lord. She wants to make people rebellious to the Lord and disobey his voice.

This spirit attracts believers and church leaders by putting greed of money and wealth, the desire of lust and women, pride of worldly status and respect in their hearts.

The spirit of Herodias using people in the churches to oppose the plans of God. This spirit is failing them to achieve their goals. Herodias used her daughter to kill John the Baptist. In the same way, the spirit of Herodias can use anything to fulfil her desire and plans. She did not even spare her daughter.

Most of the time, this spirit attacks the church leaders' families, their spouse, and their children. This spirit raises them to stand against the leader, rebel against their ideas, and disobey what they say. This spirit creates disunity in the church and family. This spirit makes people more selfish and more self-centred.

The purpose of the spirit of Herodias is to steal loyalty, obedience, care, compassion, and obedience from the families.

This spirit knows that when she succeeds in destroying the family then very quickly, she will destroy the church.

Family is a symbol of submission, unity, love, and loyalty. However, the spirit of Herodias wants to turn it into discord and a place of selfishness.

When Herodias's spirit achieves her plans and desires in the families, she uses these families to brings her evil plans into the churches to destroy the churches.

If Herodias's spirit is victorious in the families, then nobody can stop her from being successful in the churches.

That's why Jesus has warned us and taught us that if there is disagreement in the family, we need to reconcile it first before it grows out of control.

Matthew 5:23-24
"Therefore, if you are offering your gift at the altar and there remember that your brother has something against you, leave your gift there in front of the altar. First, go and be reconciled to your brother; then come and offer your gift."

When we don't settle our conflicts with other brothers and sisters, we open the door for Herodias' spirit and allow her to control and rule over our circumstances. In other words, we give her permission to fulfil her desire and plans in our bodies.

1 Corinthians 6:19
"Do you not know that your body is a temple of the Holy Spirit, who is in you, whom you have received from God? You are not on your own."

Remember, Herodias' spirit has no right or power over our bodies, but the Holy Spirit has total right and power over your body, spirit, and soul. Our bodies are the temple of God and God has entrusted us that we will use our bodies for God's glory.

Suppose you want to be set free from the spirit of

Herodias, which is disobedience and rebellion, then we need to confess before God the sins of disobedience and rebellion to our parents, pastors, church or any other person who has some kind of authority over us.

Let us decide today that we will never supress God's voice and will never resist what God is asking us to do. We will do whatever he will ask us to do; we will go wherever he will ask us to go. We will leave whatever he will ask us to leave. We will not be stubborn but obedient and loyal to God in all circumstances.

We need to bind down the spirit of disobedience and rebellion and release the spirit of total obedience and constant commitment.

THE FUNCTION OF THE SPIRIT OF REBELLION

The rebellion spirit makes us bitter, angry, stubborn, untouchable, undisciplined, argumentative, and depressed. The spirit of rebellion will alienate you from God, family, and society. It will drive you crazy and make you do crazy things like changing your gender and making you dislike the course, etc.

You will not have any control over your feelings, emotion, and ungodly desire. It will lead you to drugs, crime and restlessness.

There will be no joy or peace in your life. Your life will be meaningless to you. You will not have any purpose or vision in your life.

If you are under the influence of the spirit of rebellion, here are the things which you will do unknowingly.

You rebel against your leaders, not being faithful or loyal

to them.

You think you have more insight than the leaders. You get offended by the leaders very easily. You always seek recognition and praise from others. You think that you can be a better leader than others. You think that you are more intelligent, more anointed, and more gifted.

PRAYER

I bind and cast you out of my life in Jesus' mighty name every spirit of rebellion.

Every power that rebels against God leaves my life right now in Jesus' mighty name.

I break every yoke of the spirit of rebellion from my life.

Heavenly Father helps me not to initiate any form of rebellion. Please help me to be focused on the divine purpose you have called me.

I command the power of witchcraft, bitterness, stubbornness, undisciplined behaviours, loose your hold upon my life right now in Jesus' mighty name.

Heavenly Father, help me and give me the courage and the power of the Holy Spirit to overcome the spirit of rebellion. I renounce the spirit of rebellion and I ask you, Father, set me free from this spirit. I surrender my body, soul, and spirit to you and acknowledge you as my Lord and Saviour.

Fill my heart with the spirit of obedience right now in the name of Jesus Christ.

Amen.

CHAPTER 4
THE SPIRIT OF SERVANTHOOD AND COMPASSION (PHOEBE)

For many years, God was encouraging me to come into pastorship but every year I used to say that Lord, I will be ready by next year. But for one midnight service on 31st Dec 1999, I said, "Okay Lord, I am ready to do whatever you will ask me to do." I thought that it would take at least six to seven years to become a pastor because it was in my mind that I would go to Bible School which will take three to four years and once I finish the course, then I will assist the pastor for another two to three years. But I did not know that God had other plans in mind.

When I spoke to my pastor, he said to me that he was waiting to hear this thing from me for many years. So, after hearing this, without consulting with me, he spoke to Singapore church if I can join Asia Theological Centre for Missions and Evangelism for pastoral Leadership Training. They responded saying that they would be happy to take me for this training.

He informed me about their decision and said to me to get ready and prepare for travelling to Singapore in April. I was not willing to go leaving my wife behind but later, I decided to go anyway. In this way, I went to Singapore and completed my training.

When I came back from Singapore right after three months, our senior leadership in Singapore called back the pastor because he was a Singaporean missionary. They said that now the time had come for me to take over as I am a local trained person. I felt, I was not ready and prepared thoroughly but they motivated me and appointed me as a pastor.

When this Singaporean pastor left the church, almost 80% of the congregation left the church and only twelve to fifteen people continued to be members in the church. None of them could play any instrument, none of them could sing, none of them could lead to worship, so I was doing everything and after six months, I was utterly burned out spiritually. So, I said to God that I could not pastor this church as I was finding it very tough. As I was doing everything in the church, and I was burned out. I was ready to give up and one day God spoke to me and said to teach and train these twelve to fifteen people who were part of the church, and they will become your arms. So, I started teaching and training these people and within one year, the whole picture of the church was changed. Our church grew to 100 people. Within five years, we planted another six churches, and these twelve to fifteen people became leaders of the newly planted churches. Now, most of them are full-time pastors in different areas of Islamabad.

Romans 16:1-2
"I commend to you our sister Phoebe, a deacon of the church in Cenchrea. I ask you to receive her in the Lord in a way worthy of his people and to give her any help she may need from you, for she has been the benefactor of many people, including me."

Phoebe was the pastor of the church in Cenchrea. We don't know much about her in the New Testament. In her brief introduction, there is not much information about her.

So many people are a big blocking stone in the growth of the church. But many are a source of multiplication in the church like Phoebe, who was a leader of Cenchrea's church. The word Phoebe means 'brightness' or 'light'.

In the Epistle to Romans, Paul writes to the believers how they should treat with the ministers of God.

RECEIVE HER IN THE LORD

The first thing Paul urges the Roman believers was to receive Phoebe in the Lord in a way worthy of the saints. Keep in mind that she is the redeemed daughter of God by the blood of Jesus Christ. She is accepted in Christ and has been a servant of the Lord. Accept her as a beloved sister in Christ who has given her life for the service of the Lord.

Galatians 3:28 says,
"There is neither Jew nor Greek, slave nor free, male nor female, for you are all one in Christ Jesus."

She was the servant of the Lord so she should be worthy of double honour.

THE SPIRIT OF SERVANTHOOD AND COMPASSION (PHOEBE)

1 Timothy 5:17
"The elders who direct the affairs of the church well are worthy of double honour, especially those whose work is preaching and teaching."

Paul urges the believers to give her any help she may need from you physically, spiritually, emotionally, financially or in any other way. The labourer is worthy of his wages. Let her not suffer from any lack in her life. Support her and stand with her. God has honoured His servants, so we should also give them honour.

Paul tells the believers that Phoebe was a great help to many people, including him.

As she has been helpful to many, we should be beneficial to others.

Whoever helps others should be helped by others.

Now in these days, we need the spirit of servanthood and compassion in the church. Many people in the church want to be served, but they don't want to serve others. Instead of the spirit of servanthood and compassion, the spirit of pride and selfishness is working in the churches and that spirit is eating up the believers. That's why many people don't want to go to church. They are disappointed and discouraged.

Lord Jesus Christ wants the church, which is His bride, to be filled with the spirit of servanthood and compassion for others. The way Jesus served others while he was on the earth, in the same way, he wants us and his church to serve and bless others.

Remember! If the spirit of Christ is not working in us, then definitely the spirit of darkness, denial, pride, anger, swearing and stubbornness is working in us.

THE FUNCTION OF THE SPIRIT OF SERVANTHOOD AND COMPASSION

The spirit of servanthood cares less about the position. So, don't let the title tie you down.

The spirit of servanthood destroys self-glory and competition. The spirit of servanthood helps us to serve God with excitement, not out of duty. It helps us to become selfless.

A servant-hearted and compassionate person always lifts others, listen to them, and does not miss any opportunity of serving others. He feels the pain of other people. He sees people with the eyes of Jesus. He does not take advantage of the people. He always promotes others.

PRAYER

Father God, I acknowledge today that I am so often too focused on myself and my problems. Please help me to look beyond myself. Give me your compassion and put a servant's heart inside of me. Please help me to live for others as you have called me to do.

Father God, change me and empower me to live like Jesus. Reveal my pride, humble my attitudes, and soften my heart to serve others like Jesus.

In Jesus' mighty name, I pray.

Amen.

CHAPTER 5
THE SPIRIT OF BACKSLIDING (LOT)

One of our church ladies used to work in a foreigner's house as a cleaner and there was a Muslim man who was working as a chef. One day this Muslim man's wife was crying, and the Christian lady asked her the reason. The Muslim man's wife told her that their daughter is evil possessed, and they have taken her to many Muslim priests, but nobody could cure her. On that same day, they took her to the Muslim shrine called Bari Imam and the Muslim priest told them that if they will cut off the fingertips of her hands and feet of the girl, then she would be delivered. This Muslim lady was crying because if they will chop the fingertips of the hand and feet of their daughter then who would marry their daughter. This girl was very violent and used to eat raw meat. She used to bite their buffalos, goats, and other family members if they did not give her raw beef to eat. So, they used to bind her in chains.

When this Christian lady heard this story, she said to this Muslim family that they do not need to cut the fingertips of the hands and feet of their daughter, she suggested to them that they should try and get in touch with Christian priests, and she mentioned about us. So, they invited us to their house, and we went as a team and prayed for that girl and the same day God delivered her. She is completely healed and got married and has a son—praise, glory, and honour to God.

Genesis 13:1-13
So Abram went up from Egypt to the Negev, with his wife and everything he had, and Lot went with him. Abram had become very wealthy in livestock and silver and gold. From the Negev, he went from place to place until he came to Bethel, to the area between Bethel and Ai where his tent had been earlier and where he had first built an altar. There Abram called on the name of the Lord. Now Lot, who was moving about with Abram, also had flocks and herds and tents. But the land could not support them while they stayed together, for their possessions were so great that they were not able to stay together. And quarrelling arose between Abram's herders and Lot's. The Canaanites and Perizzites were also living in the land at that time. So, Abram said to Lot, "Let us not have any quarrelling between you and me, or between your herders and mine, for we are close relatives. Is not the whole land before you? Let's part company. If you go to the left, I'll go to the right; if you go to the right, I'll go to the left." Lot looked around and saw the whole plain of Jordan toward Zoar was well watered, like the garden of the Lord, like the land of Egypt. (This was before the Lord destroyed Sodom and Gomorrah.) So, Lot chose for himself the whole plain of the Jordan and set out toward the east. The two men

parted company: Abram lived in the land of Canaan, while Lot lived among the cities of the direct and pitched his tents near Sodom. Now the people of Sodom were wicked and were sinning greatly against the Lord.

Backsliding means giving up faith and confidence and giving up faith means giving up God or not following the commandments of God.

1 Kings 11:9 says, *"The LORD became angry with Solomon because his heart had turned away from the LORD, the God of Israel."*

NORMAL BACKSLIDING

The ordinary meaning of backsliding is losing excitement with God or leaving the interest in God. It means giving up reading the word of God, giving up fellowship with other believers or giving up sharing their faith with other people. In other terms, it means getting more interest in the things of the world.

BACKSLIDING OF THE BELIEVER

According to the Christian faith, it means that not being active or forsaking first love with God.

Revelation 2:4

"Yet I hold this against you: you have forsaken your first love."

SPIRITUAL BACKSLIDING

Spiritual backsliding means turning away from simplicity and truth of the gospel and living life according to the law and trying to be saved by good works.

Galatians 5:4 says, *"You who are trying to be justified by law have been alienated from Christ; you have fallen away from grace."*

BACKSLIDING IS A CONTINUOUS BEHAVIOUR

Nobody backslides from God immediately. It starts with small things. When people gradually start losing their interest in God and items related to God those little things make the person empty from the inside.

Lot's spirit is an excellent example of spiritual backsliding. We can learn three things from the life of Lot, which leads us to spiritual backsliding.

1. GREED

Genesis 13:10 says, *"Lot looked up and saw that the whole plain of the Jordan was well watered, like the garden of the LORD."*

First, we take our eyes off from God before we entirely turn away from God.

Most of the time, our eyes stick to the splendid things of this world.

Genesis 3:6 says that, *"when the woman saw that the fruit of the tree was good for food and pleasing to the eye and also desirable for gaining wisdom, she took some and ate it."*

Through eyes, greed penetrates our hearts and then that greed drives our lives and leads us to eternal destruction.

I know one pastor who lost everything because of his greed. Now he is no more in the ministry. He and his family are a symbol of backsliding. There were no blessings or joy in his family. He had left his wife and married his adopted daughter. He stole a lot of church money. Now he and his family are living in deep poverty. Even he cannot afford schooling to his children.

2. WRONG CHOICES

Lot made a wrong choice. Instead of choosing a mountain, he selects the valley.

Genesis 13:11 says, *"So Lot chose for himself the whole plain of the Jordan and set out towards the East. The two men parted company."*

Mountain always represents the presence of God. But Lot rejected the presence of God and chose the devil and the splendours of this world.

Remember, our one small wrong decision can bring big distraction in our lives. Most of the times, we give more value to the worldly possessions rather than spiritual blessings. Instead of giving glory and honour to God, we run after our benefits. Instead of thinking about the growth of the church, we think about what we can get out of it.

Our every single decision, which does not glorify the name of the Lord, becomes a stumbling block in our lives. Instead of growing spiritually, we become stagnant. Then we pretend that we are growing, but we are dying spiritually day by day.

3. COMPROMISE

Lot pitched up to his tent near Sodom.

Genesis 13:12-13

"Abram lived in the land of Canaan, while Lot lived among the

cities of the plain and pitched his tents near Sodom. Now the men of Sodom were wicked and were sinning greatly against the LORD."

Sodom was the devil's dwelling place and Lot compromised to live near Sodom. Many people say that if their friends are wicked, then that is their problem and matter. Their evil ways don't bother them. But the Bible says in 1 Corinthians 15:33, *"Don't be misled: bad company corrupts good character."* Because of the compromise of Lot, his whole family was destroyed. His wife became the pillar of salt and his two daughters had sex with him and in this way polluted the relationship of father and daughter.

Always remember that whatever you do good or bad, it still produces fruit. If you have done something right, then it will produce good fruit but if you have done something wrong, then it will produce bad fruit. If we meet with good people, then we will become good people but if we mix up with wrong people, indeed we will be influenced by them and gain their bad characteristics.

HOW DOES THE SPIRIT OF BACKSLIDING WORK?

The spirit of backsliding works very slowly, No one turns away from God overnight. The spirit of backsliding first steals our love with God and then our interest in the things which pleases God, little by little and day by day. With time, it completely takes over us. Here are the things which please God and the spirit of backsliding steal it from our lives.

1. CEASING PRAYER

Prayer is an excellent weapon against the powers of the darkness. Satan is not afraid of anything except the prayers of a righteous man; that's why the devil put all his efforts and energy to stop Christians from praying.

Prayer is spiritual breathing for a righteous man. As we breathe naturally to survive, in the same way, we need spiritual breathing for living spiritually.

By praying, we put ourselves according to the will of God. Ceasing prayer is a kind of pride that stops us from coming into the presence of God.

Remember! The activities or things which keep us busy and stop us from praying become the real cause of spiritual defeat and backsliding.

2. STOP READING THE WORD OF GOD

God speaks to us through His Word and when we stop reading the Word of God, then we stop listening to the voice of God. Then it becomes a significant cause of our backsliding and spiritual defeat.

When we reject the word of God, we deny the voice of God. Denying the voice of God is hardening our hearts, which is sin. Sin separates us from God and his people. The wages of sin are death which is separation from God.

3. STOP GOING TO CHURCH

When we go to church, we defeat the devil on our doorstep in our homes. The devil always wants to stop us from going to church. The devil knows that when these people go to church, they will get power from God against him.

So when the devil keeps the people bound in their houses, he weakens them spiritually. So, the devil is not afraid of weak Christians.

By going to church, we learn to live a victorious life, that's why the writer of the Hebrews says that, *"Let us not give up meeting together as some are in the habit of doing."* (Hebrews 10:25)

4. DISOBEYING THE HOLY SPIRIT
Holy Spirit is our teacher, and he is always there to teach us, direct us and discipline us. When we stop following the instructions of the Holy Spirit, then our action leads us to spiritual laziness and backsliding.

Ephesians 4:30 says that,
"And do not grieve the Holy Spirit of God, with whom you were sealed for the day of redemption."

5. NOT LIVING A LIFE ACCORDING TO THE WORD OF GOD
Psalms 119:105 says that,
"Your word is a lamp to my feet and a light for my path."

The person who doesn't walk in the light of the lamp always stumbled and the person who consistently stumbles cannot walk properly and the person who cannot walk properly cannot reach his destination.

If you think the spirit of Lot which is the spirit of backsliding is taking you in it's grips little by little and you are slipping away from the first love of God and sweet fellowship of the Holy Spirit, then you need to come back to God and need to confess your stubbornness. Ask God to forgive you for your laziness and restore your first love with Him. Ask God to restore your excitement and fill your heart with a new love for HIM. Ask God to give you strength so that you can stop going towards backsliding behaviours.

Today commit with your Lord God that you will read the word of God every day. You will spend more time with God in prayer. You will grow in fellowship with other believers. You will obey and follow the instructions of the Holy Spirit and you will give priority in your life to the Holy Spirit. You will live your life according to the Word of God.

Remember! God wants to help us to overcome our backsliding behaviours. Jeremiah 3:22 says that,

"Return, faithless people; I will cure you of backsliding."

And then Hosea 14:4 says that,

"I will heal their waywardness and love them freely, for my anger has turned away from them."

Let us pray for the perfect restoration and blessings of the real Christian life. Pray that we always live free from the control of the spirit of backsliding.

THE FUNCTION OF THE SPIRIT OF BACKSLIDING

Backsliding is leaving God and following the worldly desires and lifestyle. In other words, backsliding is sliding downwards away from the Lordship of Christ.

In backsliding, our spiritual growth stops, and we begin to trend downward. Backsliding looks like gratifying the desires of the flesh instead of living according to the Holy Spirit.

Backsliding is living in the flesh and the acts of the flesh are sexual immorality, impurity, debauchery, idolatry, witchcraft, hatred, discord, jealousy, fits of rage, selfish ambitions, dissension, factions, envy, drunkenness, and orgies. (Galatians 5:19-20)

Backsliding is like lukewarmness to the things of Christ. (Revelation 3:16)

Backsliding is putting one's hand to the plough and looking back. (Luke 9:62)

Backsliding is like a dog returning to its vomit. (Proverbs 26:11, 2 Peter 2:22)

Backsliding is like a salt losing its flavour. (Matthew 5:13 Backsliding is turning away from God. (1 Kings 11:9)

The spirit of backsliding puts spiritual pride inside of us. This spirit kills hunger for the Word of God from our lives. This spirit steals the desire for prayer from our hearts.

The spirit of backsliding increases worldly desires inside of us. It motivates us that giving more time in playing games and sports, watching favourite TV programs, or engaging in recreational activities than prayer, Bible Study or other spiritual activities are not sin.

The spirit of backsliding gives us justifications of sins and steals the sense of godliness and throw us into the pit of guilt and shame. This spirit encourages us that we do not need to repent from our sins.

The spirit of backsliding gradually takes away a Christian from the church and integrates him with the world until he completely follows the worldly desires and lust.

Under the influence of this spirit, the heart first withdraws from God before a Christian begins to withdraw from fellowship with other believers.

PRAYER

Father, I come to you in the name of Jesus Christ. I confess that I have fallen away from you. I acknowledge that I have sinned against you by backsliding away from you, your ways, and your word. I repent and turn away from this evil life that I have lived.

Today I commit my life to you. I want you to be the Lord of my life now and forevermore. Lord of my mind and all my attitudes and my mental health. Lord of my body and my physical health. Lord of my spirit and all my worship. Lord of my family and all my relationships. Lord of my sexuality and its expression. Lord of all my work and service for you. Lord of all my material goods and needs. Lord of all my finances. Lord of all my emotions and all my reactions. Lord of my will and all my decisions. Lord of my manner and time of my death.

Heavenly Father fill me once again with your Holy Spirit that I might live unto righteousness with you. Restore me into fellowship with you.

Lord Jesus Christ, you are the baptiser of the Holy Spirit. I ask for a fresh infilling of the Holy Spirit so that I might live for you all the days of my life in power and authority. Lord restores my life and the fellowship we once shared. Lord root out the darkness and light up my life with your holy presence.

In Jesus' mighty name, I pray.

Amen

CHAPTER 6
THE SPIRIT OF FAITHFULNESS (BEZALEL)

GOD BLESSED ME WITH A CAR

One day my wife, my daughter Naysa and I went to visit my mother in Islamabad. When we wanted to leave, my mother asked my youngest brother - Binyamin to drop us home in his car. Binyamin refused and said that as I am a pastor, I need to pray to my God, and He can provide me a car. But I said to my mother not to worry as we would take a taxi. We walked to the supermarket and waited for a taxi for almost three hours and on that day, nobody was willing to go to Iqbal Town, where we were living. While we were standing in front of the United Bakery, it was raining and after three hours my mother called me and asked me if we reached home safely? I told her that still we are standing in front of the United Bakery and waiting for a taxi because nobody wanted to go to Iqbal Town. That was the time when God touched my mother's heart. As soon as I finished talking to her, a taxi came and I told the driver that we want to go to Iqbal Town and he was willing to go and within half an hour we reached our home in Iqbal Town.

The next morning, my mother called me and asked me to come over to her place. So, in the afternoon, I went to see her, and she gave me PKR (Pakistani Rupees) Rs. 100,000 (£1300.0) and asked me to get a car by lease from the bank. So just within one month, I got my new car—praise, glory, and honour to God.

GOD BLESSED US WITH A HOUSE

While I was pastoring a church in Islamabad, we used to live in church property, but when the church asked us to move from that property, we did not have any place to live, and the house rent was very high which we could not afford. So, we were moved from Calvary Charismatic Church building to Iqbal Town. This house was my mother's property and she had built this house for herself. My mother was a beautician and she had bought the property for all our brothers. She had purchased a piece of land for me as well. So, when we were living in my mother's house, one day my youngest brother Binyamin asked my mother that since William is a pastor, he might not have sufficient money to build his house. So, take his piece of land and give him your built home. My mother agreed to the proposal as my part of the land was more significant than the place where we were living. So, when they talked to me, I was happy because I knew that I would not be able to construct my own house. So, in this way, I swapped my piece of land with the built home.

PROVISION IN SINGAPORE

When I was studying in Singapore, the college dean said to all the married students that if their wives want to visit them in Singapore, they can come during the break. So, I called my local church in Islamabad and asked them if they can sponsor my wife and daughter. They told me that they are not able to support my wife and daughter, so they declined. Then I talked to my mother and asked her if she can sponsor them. She said to me to call her back after three days. So, I did, and she also refused. Then I was very disappointed but prayed and said to God that you could do everything, and nothing is impossible for you. So, I started praying almost every day for the provision and one day I was going from Tempnies to Toa Payoh and God spoke to me and said to me, "Do you love me more than your wife?" I said "Yes, Lord, you know that I love you more than anything else."

So He said to me "If I provide you with all the money you need for your wife and daughter to come to Singapore, will you return it to me?" I said, "Okay God. If you provide all this money tomorrow (Sunday), then I will return it to you, but if you deliver on Monday, then I will not return it to you." This was my deal with God.

I thought that it is a considerable amount and how can I get all that money in one day. It would be impossible.

The next day, when I was worshipping in the church, a steward came and handed over an envelope to me and said to me that somebody handed this envelope to be given to me. So, I took that envelope and put it in my right-hand side trouser pocket. After some time, another steward came, and he gave me another envelope and told me that somebody had given him that envelope for me. So, I took that envelope from him and put it in my left-hand side trouser pocket. So, while I was worshipping a third steward came with the third envelope and said the same statement. So, I took that third envelope from him and kept it in the front pocket of my shirt. I was amazed by what God was doing. To my left side there was an empty seat and a man sat down but I thought that maybe he also had brought another envelope.

So after the church service, I went to the coffee shop and opened all those envelopes one by one. When I opened the first envelope there was Singapore $1000, in the second envelope there was S$1000 and when I opened the third envelope there was S$500. That was the exact amount that I needed for my wife and daughter to get them to Singapore. Then I decided to give all that money back to God for mission work on the same day in the evening service. Our God is promise-keeping God and always. He is faithful with his people who trust in Him.

Exodus 35:30-33
"Then Moses said to the Israelites, "See, the Lord has chosen Bezalel son of Uri, the son of Hur, of the tribe of Judah and he has filled him with the Spirit of God, with wisdom, with understanding, with knowledge and with all kinds of skills—to make artistic designs for work in gold, silver and bronze, to cut and set stones, to work in wood and to engage in all kinds of artistic crafts."

Bezalel was not a prophet, not a priest, or not a leader. He was an ordinary man who was filled with the Spirit of God, with skills, abilities, knowledge in all kinds of crafts to make artistic design for work in gold, silver and bronze to cut and set stones, to work in wood and to engage in all kinds of artistic craftsmanship.

God chose Bezalel from the tribe of Judah (Exodus 31:1) so that he will make all the things required for the tabernacle. God filled him with the spirit, with the skills, the ability and knowledge in all kinds of crafts because God knew that we could not do anything without his Holy Spirit.

BEZALEL MADE THE TABERNACLE

He made the ten curtains for the tabernacle. Each curtain was the same size - twenty-eight cubits long four cubits wide. (Exodus 36:9)

He made the tent over the tabernacle with curtains of goat hair. He made eleven curtains for this purpose.

All eleven curtains were the same size - thirty cubits long and four cubits wide. (Exodus 36:14-15)

BEZALEL MADE THE ARK

Bezalel made the Ark of acacia wood - two and a half cubits long, a cubit and a half wide and a cubit half high. He overlaid it with pure gold, both inside and out and made an excellent moulding around it. (Exodus 37:1-2)

BEZALEL MADE THE TABLE

"He made the Table of Acacia wood - two cubits long, a cubit wide and a cubit and a half high. Then they overlaid it with pure gold and a gold moulding around it." (Exodus 37:10-11)

BEZALEL MADE THE LAMPSTAND
He made the lampstand of pure gold. He made the lampstand and all its accessories from one talent of pure gold. (Exodus 37:17)

BEZALEL MADE THE ALTAR OF INCENSE
Bezalel made the Altar of Incense out of Acacia wood. It was square, a cubit long and a cubit wide and two cubits high. (Exodus 37:25)

BEZALEL MADE THE ANOINTING OIL AND THE INCENSE
Bezalel made the sacred anointing oil and the pure fragrant incense blended as by the perfumer.

BEZALEL MADE THE ALTAR OF THE BURNT OFFERING
Bezalel built the Altar for burnt offering of acacia wood, three cubits high; it was square, five cubits long and five cubits wide.

BEZALEL MADE THE PRIESTLY GARMENTS
From the blue, purple and scarlet yarn He made woven garments for ministering in the sanctuary. He also made sacred garments for Aaron, as the LORD commanded Moses.

Whatever the talents and abilities God has given to us, God can use it for his glory, but the condition is that we do it wholeheartedly and faithfully. Whatever we are doing in our lives, can bring glory and honour to God irrespective of whether it is big or small. Bezalel was not a spiritual leader, but still, God used him for his purpose. He did the work which many spiritual leaders could not do. The word of the Lord says that whatever you do, do it for the Lord.

Whatever you do in your life, God wants you to be faithful in that whether it is your job, business, study or doing your everyday household chores. If you are sincere and loyal in what you are doing for God, He will bless you with more.

If you are sincere and faithful in the worldly things then definitely you will be honest and loyal in the spiritual things.

Bezalel was sincere and faithful in all his doings; that's why God called him by his name and chose him for the work of His house.

In these days, the spirit of faithfulness is missing from the churches. People are not faithful to God, their church and even with other believers.

Bezalel made the Ark of the Covenant thousands of years ago, but still, we remember him. In the same way, whatever we will do faithfully will remain as a memorial for hundreds of years.

If the spirit of faithfulness is not working in us then the spirit of performance, the spirit of selfishness, the spirit of achievement and the spirit of self-motivation is working which are doing things not pleasing to God but to glorify our self-image and ego.

THE FUNCTION OF THE SPIRIT OF FAITHFULNESS

The spirit of faithfulness compels us to submit ourselves to God and His Holy Spirit. It comes from a place of realising that we need a Saviour and that He is in control of our lives. The spirit of faithfulness keeps us loyal to God and keeps us dependent on God.

THE SPIRIT OF FAITHFULNESS (BEZALEL)

The spirit of faithfulness gives us the ability to decide to stand with God, to trust completely in Him, to remain committed to Him, even when life is hard, even when life is 'on the edge'.

PRAYER

Lord, I ask you to please make me a faithful servant who will remain loyal to you always.

Heavenly Father teach me to be the servant you have called me to be. Please help me to stand firm in my faith no matter how difficult the road becomes.

Help me cling to you as my anchor. Help me remember, your steadfast love and faithfulness for me in all things.

In Jesus mighty name, I pray.

Amen.

CHAPTER 7
THE SPIRIT OF DISBELIEF AND RELIGION (ESAU)

GOD PROVIDED FOR A CHURCH BUILDING

A few years ago, some of our church leaders came to me and said that they wanted to have their worship in a proper church building as we used to worship in a tent. Their children didn't want to come to church because of the heat inside the tent. In Pakistan, summer is sweltering and sometimes the temperature can go up to 52 degrees Celsius. They said to me that they have only two choices. Either we must have our church building or they would go to another church. I told them that getting our church building is not very difficult. If they were willing to sacrifice, we can have our church building just within a few months. They were delighted and they said to me that whatever I would tell them, they will do it. So next week, I built a wall with 100 blocks and numbered each block from starting from 1 at the bottom to 100 at the top, in front of the pulpit and told them that this is a Jericho wall. When you break this wall, then you will be able to enter your church building as the Israelites entered the Promised Land. I told them that each blocks value is Rs. 5,000 (£45) which was equal to one month's salary at that time. Praise, glory, and honour to God that just within three months this whole wall was removed, and we had raised Rs. 500,000 (£2,950).

One day, I had shown a video in the church called 'Jewels Falling from Heaven' – about jewels that had fallen in the church in Puerto Rico. One of the pastors, who came from the village, when he watched this video started praying, "God! If you can give diamonds to the white people, can you not give us gold?" He used to pray in this way whenever he remembered this video. One day he was going back home from the cell group meeting on his motorbike when he saw something reflecting from the ground. He stopped his bike to have a look. He was amazed to see four gold stones weighing almost 100g. Following Sunday, he testified in church and said that he wanted to give that gold towards the church building fund. But I told him that since he was also planning to build a church building in his village, he had more need of it and keep it with him and this will be a testimony for his church members too.

So one of my assistant pastors who was present there, when he heard this testimony said to himself that if God can give gold then He can provide with diamonds as well. One day he was going to his office on his bicycle. While cycling, one of his tyres brushed past a small box. He ignored it, but later a thought came in his mind to go back and check what was in that box. So, he cycled back and when he investigated that box, there was a white gold ring with six diamond studs on top of it. He came next Sunday in the church and testified. He gave that six diamond studs white gold ring for the church building fund.

When I preached about the Jericho wall in the church, a week later a widow from our church came to me and said, "Pastor, I have saved this money for my son's wedding. Please take it and build the house of the Lord and God will arrange for my son's wedding." She gave Rs. 50,000 (£290). One and half years later, her son got married and God provided everything abundantly, after paying for all expenses she had Rs.100,000 (£560) remaining. Our God is a miracle-working God.

Within one year, we bought a piece of land, constructed the church building and dedicated it to the LORD.

Hebrews 12:16-17

"See that no one is sexually immoral, or is godless like Esau, who for a single meal, sold his inheritance rights as the oldest son. Afterwards, as you know, when he wanted to inherit this blessing, he was rejected. Even though he sought the blessing with tears, he could not change what he had done."

Esau was walking under the spirit of disbelief and religion. Under the spirit of religion, people know the traditions in their minds and follow them out worldly, but they do not understand the true meaning of the rules and do not accept them from their hearts.

Esau knew the blessings and the value of the firstborn, but

THE SPIRIT OF DISBELIEF AND RELIGION (ESAU)

he still despised the right of the firstborn. He sold his birth right for the sake of one meal.

Esau knew the commandments of God and the promises God made with Abraham and Isaac. However, he still disowned the promises and commandments of God and worried about his life. Maybe he thought that if he died of starvation then what would he do with his birth right.

Let us see Genesis 24:29-34,
"Once when Jacob was cooking some stew, Esau came in from the open country, famished. He said to Jacob, "Quick, let me have some of that red stew! I am famished!" Jacob replied, "First sell me your birth right."

"Look, I am about to die," Esau said, "What good is the birth right to me?" But Jacob said," Swear to me first." So, he swore an oath to him, selling his birth right to Jacob. Then Jacob gave Esau some bread and some lentil stew. He ate and drank and then got up and left. So, Esau abandoned his birth right."

RELIGIOUS PEOPLE LOSE THEIR SPIRITUAL BLESSINGS
Esau said to his father," Do you have only one blessing, my Father? Bless me too, my father!" Then Esau wept aloud. (Genesis 27:38)

Esau wept out loud because he had lost his chance to be blessed.

These days, the spirit of Esau is working very powerfully in the churches, which are the spirit of disbelief and religion.

People know Christ, but they do not follow him wholeheartedly. People know about Christ, but they don't accept him as their Lord and Saviour. People see the value and power of the blood of Jesus, but they don't cover themselves with the blood of Jesus. People know about the sacrificial death of Christ, but they do not accept it for their lives.

So in this way, they lose all their spiritual, physical, and material blessings.

People are dying without Christ, families are getting destroyed and society is demoralised because people are focused on being more religious than to have a relationship with God.

Spirit of religion binds us into the rituals and traditions.

RELIGIOUS PEOPLE CANNOT ENTER THE KINGDOM OF GOD

On the Day of Judgment, many people will face Jesus, who will not be great sinners, but they will be excellent and good people. They will be people who were more religious rather than spiritual.

They followed religion rather than having a relationship with God. Christianity is not a religion; it is a relationship. Religious people offer their prayers, read their bible, go to church and meet with other believers, out of their duties or fear that if they do not do all these things, then God will be angry with them.

Many religious people claim that they are serving God, they are prophesying, casting out demons and doing great and mighty things for the Lord, but they have no relationship with God. Their hearts are far away from God. They are just using the name of Jesus Christ.

There is power in the name of Jesus Christ and any person

THE SPIRIT OF DISBELIEF AND RELIGION (ESAU)

can use this power and authority.

We know through the scriptures that some people used the power and authority of the name of Jesus Christ.

Let us read Acts 19:13-16,
"Some Jews who went around driving out evil spirits tried to invoke the name of the Lord Jesus over those who were demon-possessed. They would say, "In the name of the Jesus whom Paul preaches, I command you to come out." Seven sons of Sceva, a Jewish chief priest, were doing this. One day the evil spirit answered them, "Jesus I know, and Paul I know about, but who are you?" Then the man who had the evil spirit jumped on them and overpowered them all. He gave them such a beating that they ran out of the house naked and bleeding."

When religious people use the power and name of Jesus Christ, they never always succeed. Religious people do all these things to glorify their names and raise their profile. They perform rituals and are stuck in the routines. They do not talk about the intimacy with God but always talk about the miracles or the dos and don'ts.

Jesus says to these kinds of religious people to go away from Him as He does not know them.

These kinds of people will not be able to enter the kingdom of God. Religious people always run after the gifts of the Holy Spirit rather than the fruit of the Holy Spirit.

Religious people cannot establish a great intimacy with God. Holy Spirit gives us the gifts of the Holy Spirit but the fruit of the Holy Spirit; we produce in our lives by ourselves. So that's why God doesn't look for gifts of the Holy Spirit in our lives, but he looks for the fruit of the Holy Spirit.

Religion people know about God, but they neither glorify Him nor give thanks to Him. They run after their spiritual desires.

They pray, but their hearts are stuck in the worldly and lustful desires.

They go to church, but they criticise pastors and other believers. They judge others and do all these ungodly things out of their carnal nature which they have not submitted to God. They trust in their good works and believe that they will please God with their good works.

Remember! Religious people cannot please God, nor they can have a real relationship with God.

John 1:12-13 says that,
"Yet to all who received him, to those who believe in his name, he gave the right to become children of God, children born not of natural descent, nor human decision or a husband's will, but born of God."

Religious people always live in fear that God will get angry with them. Religious people always try to control their feelings and emotions. Religious people are stuck in sin and repentance trap. They don't grow furthermore.

Today, we need to examine ourselves; are we living under the spirit of religion?

If we are living under the spirit of religion, then we need to confess of it and need to surrender our lives to Jesus Christ once again.

THE SPIRIT OF DISBELIEF AND RELIGION (ESAU)

The spirit of Esau is working in the churches very powerfully, which is the spirit of religion, the spirit of performance, the spirit of rejection, the orphan spirit and the spirit of selfishness. We need to bind these spirits down in the name of Jesus Christ. We need to ask for God's forgiveness. We need to ask God to set us free from these spirits.

If we do not set ourselves free from the control of these spirits, then we will become like Esau who lost his relationship with Israelites and as well as with God. In the same way, if we are not aware of it, then we will also lose our relationship with our heavenly Father.

THE FUNCTION OF THE RELIGIOUS SPIRIT

The religious spirit places ungodly limitations upon people's lives and tries to mask their identity.

The people bound by the religious spirit are more of the murmuring, complaining and wrong speaking nature. They are dry in relationships and lacking the life of God.

The most prominent action of the religious spirit is a critical attitude. Under the influence of this spirit, people enjoy debate and disagreements, which leads to endless disputes. Their attitude and mindset are more negative rather than positive.

The religious spirit emphasises more on works without the power of the Holy Spirit and opens the door to compromise.

The religious spirit continually harasses and condemns people. The religious spirit always limits the spirit of God.

PRAYER

Father, in the name of Jesus Christ, I come before you and

ask you to deliver me from the spirit of religion and help me to have an intimate relationship with you. Please help me to have a real revelation of you who you are.

I repent and renounce every spirit of religion or religious spirit and every work of darkness connected with it.

I renounce the belief that you are distant, unkind or judgemental.

I repent and renounce all legalism, traditions and religious formulas I have followed or practised.

I repent and renounce all comparison, judgment, criticism, gossip, envy and anger.

Heavenly Father, wash me and cleanse me, from all the sins I have confessed and renounced with the blood of Jesus Christ. Please help me to live as a son, not as a slave.

I proclaim that all that is good and blessed of God, all that is in the perfect will of God, all that God has designed for me shall come to me in Jesus' mighty name.

The spirit of truth is in me. He gives me divine wisdom, divine direction, divine understanding of every situation and every circumstance of life. I have the wisdom of God.

I thank you, Father, that the Spirit of God leads me. I have the mind of Christ and the wisdom of God is within me.

In Jesus' mighty name, I pray.

Amen.

CHAPTER 8
THE SPIRIT OF PERFECT OBEDIENCE AND SUBMISSION (MARY)

HOW I STARTED 'GO AND SAVE MINISTRIES'
When I came to know Jesus on 30th September 1994, my life was utterly changed, and I wanted to tell everybody what Jesus has done for me.

January 1996, I read a book called 'God's Smugglers' written by Brother Andrew founder of Open Doors. Before I finished this book, God spoke to me that I need to do something like Brother Andrew. As I was reading this book, I felt that God's plan was revealed to me. When I finished this book, I couldn't sleep for many nights. Almost every night God was saying the same thing again and again, but I was not daring enough to take this responsibility, or maybe I didn't know how to do what God was calling me to do.

I struggled with the thoughts for two months. Meanwhile, I shared what God was saying to me with my friends. My friend Sohail was agreeing to do whatever I wanted to do.

On 6th March 1996, with some of my pocket money, I made some photocopies of the leaflet called 'Four things which God wants you to know' and distributed it in the streets of the Islamabad. After distributing these leaflets, the joy God gave us cannot be described in words.

That was the beginning of the 'Go & Save' ministry.

God blessed and multiplied this ministry and in a couple of years, it turned to Go and Save Islamabad to Go & Save Pakistan. Under this ministry, we started adult education schools, trained young leaders for Muslim evangelism and distributed gospel to every single house in Islamabad.

In this ministry, all aged people were involved - young, old, youth, men, and women. In my country, it is not common for young girls and women to go for literature distribution but in Go and Save, all went out.

On many occasions police arrested us, put us in lock up, Muslims stoned, beaten, verbally abused us but every time the joy of the Lord and mercy of the Lord was incredible and beyond our understanding.

Praise, glory, thanks, and honour to our God Father for everything He has done.

Luke 1:26-55
"In the sixth month of Elizabeth's pregnancy, God sent the angel Gabriel to Nazareth, a town in Galilee, to a virgin pledged to be married to a man named Joseph, a descendant of David. The virgin's name was Mary. The angel went to her and said, "Greetings, you who are highly favoured! The Lord is with you."

Mary was greatly troubled at his words and wondered what

THE SPIRIT OF PERFECT OBEDIENCE AND SUBMISSION (MARY)

kind of greeting this might be. But the angel said to her, "Do not be afraid, Mary; you have found favour with God. You will conceive and give birth to a son, and you are to call him Jesus. He will be great and will be called the Son of the Most High. The Lord God will give him the throne of his father David and he will reign over Jacob's descendants forever; his kingdom will never end."

"How will this be," Mary asked the angel, "since I am a virgin?"

The angel answered, "The Holy Spirit will come on you and the power of the Most High will overshadow you. So, the holy one to be born will be called the Son of God. Even Elizabeth, your relative, is going to have a child in her old age and she who was said to be unable to conceive is in her sixth month. For no word from God will ever fail."

"I am the Lord's servant," Mary answered. "May your word to me be fulfilled." Then the angel left her.

At that time Mary got ready and hurried to a town in the hill country of Judea, where she entered Zechariah's home and greeted Elizabeth. When Elizabeth heard Mary's greeting, the baby leapt in her womb and Elizabeth was filled with the Holy Spirit. In a loud voice, she exclaimed: "Blessed, are you among women and blessed is the child you will bear! But why am I so favoured that the mother of my Lord should come to me? As soon as the sound of your greeting reached my ears, the baby in my womb leapt for joy. Blessed is she who has believed that the Lord would fulfil his promises to her!"

And Mary said:

"My soul glorifies the Lord, and my spirit rejoices in God, my Saviour, for he has been mindful of the humble state of his

servant. From now on, all generations will call me blessed, for the Mighty One has done great things for me, holy is his name. His mercy extends to those who fear him, from generation to generation. He has performed mighty deeds with his arm; He has scattered those who are proud in their innermost thoughts. He has brought down rulers from their thrones but has lifted the humble. He has filled the hungry with good things but has sent the rich away empty. He has helped his servant Israel, remembering to be merciful to Abraham and his descendants forever, just as he promised our ancestors."

Mary, the mother of Jesus, was chosen by God for the redemption of the whole of humankind. She had the spirit of perfect obedience and total submission; that's why she gave her life to God used for his plan and purpose.

Mary was an ordinary woman of blood and flesh, but her total submission and complete obedience made her unique and supernatural woman. Her decision made her an extraordinary woman.

Let us see some of the qualities of the life of Mary.

SHE WAS A VIRGIN

God gave a special grace and favour which nobody had got in this world apart from her. The virgin birth never happened in this world before her. No woman has conceived without human contact. She gave birth to a son, and he was born under the law.

Galatians 4:4 says,
"But when the time had fully come, God sent his Son, born of

THE SPIRIT OF PERFECT OBEDIENCE AND SUBMISSION (MARY)

a woman, born under the law."

Jesus Christ was born according to the will of God, according to the plan of God and precisely the way God wanted.

The Son, who was born by Mary, was born as the seed of the woman.

Genesis 3:15 says,
"And I will put enmity between you and the woman and between your offspring and hers; he will crush your head and you will strike his heel."

She gave birth to a son, and he was born by the power of the Holy Spirit.

Matthew 1:20 says,
"But after he had considered this, an angel of the Lord appeared to him in a dream and said, "Joseph son of David, do not be afraid to take Mary home as your wife, because what conceived in her is from the Holy Spirit."

GOD HAS GIVEN HER SPECIAL STATUS AND HONOUR

God has given Mary a special status and respect. It is not a normal status, honour, or privilege to be a mother of the Saviour of the world or to be used for the plan of the salvation of the whole world.

There are so many misunderstandings regarding the status, honour, and privilege of Mary; she had this from the Lord. Many people think that she is a mediator between man and God because Jesus was born through her. Jesus is God and that's why Mary is called the mother of God.

But we need to remember that Jesus was a perfect man and perfect God. For being God, he didn't need to be born from a woman. But as a man, he needs to be delivered from a woman. So, Mary is the mother of Jesus Christ as a perfect man but not as a perfect God.

Remember, Mary is not a god. She was a human being like you and me. She said about herself that *"I am the LORD'S servant."* (Luke 1:38)

Roman Catholic people say that Mary is mother of God. We need to remember that human gives birth to humans, animals give birth to animals, birds give birth to birds and a spirit gives birth to a spirit. When Jesus said that God prepared flesh for me, he was referring to his human birth. A human body can form in the mother's womb. Another thing which we need to remember is that God is spirit, and He has no physical body like human beings.

MARY BELIEVED IN THE WORD OF GOD, WHOLEHEARTEDLY

Mary obeyed and surrendered to the Word of God. Let us see some of the characteristics of the life of Mary, which makes her an extraordinary woman. It lifts her from the level of an ordinary woman.

1. Mary was a prayerful woman.

ACTS 1:14

"They joined together constantly in prayer, along with the woman and Mary, the mother of Jesus and with his brothers."

THE SPIRIT OF PERFECT OBEDIENCE AND SUBMISSION (MARY)

2. Mary believed in the supernatural power of God.

LUKE 1:38
"I am the Lord's servant," Mary answered, "may it be to me as you have said," then the angel left her. She said, "may it be to me as you have said."

3. Mary surrendered herself to God.
She accepted the will of God and said that bear unto me according to the Word of God. (Luke 1:38)

4. Mary was a true worshipper. Luke 1:46-55
She worshipped the Lord and said that my soul glorifies the Lord, and my spirit rejoices in God, my Saviour because he has done great things for me. His name is holy, and he extends his mercy to those who fear him. He has lifted the humble. He has filled the hungry with good things. He has remembered to be merciful from generation to generation. (Luke 1:46-55)

5. Mary used to meditate on the Word of God.

LUKE 2:19
"But Mary treasured up all these things and pondered them in her heart."

Pondering on the Word of God is a symbol of a dedicated and mature believer. We live a victorious life by the power of his word, which works in us always.

6. Mary used to go to the house of the Lord. She knew the value of the house of the Lord. She used to go to the house of the Lord every year. (Luke 2:41-52)

Luke 2:41-42
"Every year his parents went to Jerusalem for the feast of the Passover. When he was twelve years old, they went up to the feast, according to the custom."

Mary was an ordinary woman made of blood and flesh, but because of her complete surrender and obedience, she gave that respect, honour, and privilege which nobody else has got.

Because of her gentle, obedient, and loyal spirit, she became a great and supernatural woman.

She gained that honour and respect which no one else has got apart from her.

If we allow the spirit of perfect obedience and surrender to work in our lives, then we will be able to achieve astonishing and mighty things for God.

If we are obedient to the Word of God like Mary, then God will take us to the highest levels of this world. He will give us all our heart's desires. He will bless us beyond our imagination.

But there is a condition; if we commit ourselves into the hands of God, surrender all to him and follow him with all our heart, then he will not set aside any blessing from us. He will rain his grace and mercy on us.

Let the spirit of real commitment, the spirit of perfect obedience, the spirit of total submission, discipline and surrender work in us.

THE SPIRIT OF PERFECT OBEDIENCE AND SUBMISSION (MARY)

If the spirit of total obedience is not working inside of us, then it means that the spirit of disobedience is working in us. Half obedience is equal to total disobedience.

If we do not surrender, then it means that we have the force inside us, which compels us to resist the godly things.

If we are not walking according to the Word of God, then it means that we are walking according to the will and plan of Satan.

If we are not following the truth, then it means that we are pursuing lies and deception. We need to examine ourselves, how we are walking, and which spirit is working inside of us – the spirit of Christ or the spirit of darkness.

THE FUNCTION OF THE SPIRIT OF OBEDIENCE AND SUBMISSION

The spirit of obedience and submission helps us to worship God in spirit and truth because obedience and submission are an act of worship.

The spirit of obedience proves our love for God. The spirit of obedience demonstrates our faith in God. The Word of God says that obedience is better than sacrifice. Obedience helps us to have an intimate relationship with God. Through obedience, we experience the blessings of God physically, spiritually, worldly, emotionally, and financially.

The spirit of obedience helps us to walk with God in confidence. The spirit of obedience allows us to obey the voice of God and strengthen us to overcome every kind of fear.

PRAYER

Father in the name of Jesus Christ today, I renounce

the spirit of disobedience in my life. I acknowledge and declare that I belong to the Lord Jesus Christ, and I am the sheep of His pasture. I obey the Lord's voice regularly and consistently. I invite the spirit of obedience and submission into my life in Jesus mighty name.

Amen.

CHAPTER 9
THE SPIRIT OF DECEPTION (JUDAS)

MY WIFE LOST HER PURSE
Once, my wife lost her purse and all her cards like national ID, driving license, bank cards and some money too. She was agitated because it is cumbersome to get a replacement card and sometimes it takes ages. When she told me, I asked the intercessors, "Please pray that the person who has this purse takes all the money but sends the cards back." We prayed as well that Lord sends your angel to bring all the cards back to us. It is common in my country Pakistan, for people to take all the money and throw away the cards in the rubbish. We kept on praying and after three days, my wife received all her cards through the mail. Glory and praise to God. Our God is faithful.

Matthew 27:1-5
"Early in the morning, all the chief priests and the elders of the people made their plans on how to have Jesus executed. So they bound him, led him away and handed him over to Pilate,

the governor.

When Judas, who had betrayed him, saw that Jesus condemned, he was seized with remorse and returned the thirty pieces of silver to the chief priests and the elders. "I have sinned," he said, "for I have betrayed innocent blood."

"What is that to us?" they replied. "That's your responsibility."

So Judas threw the money into the temple and left. Then he went away and hanged himself."

Love and friendship refresh our souls. But if a friend or loved one deceives or betrays then that deception leaves unhealed wounds in our heart and soul which even doctors cannot heal.

These wounds can be healed only by the love, loyalty, and faithfulness of the friend.

Jesus chose twelve disciples to accomplish the plan and purpose of God on earth. These disciples followed Jesus wherever he went and whatever he did.

Judas Iscariot was one of them.

THE CHARACTER OF JUDAS ISCARIOT

Jesus chose Judas Iscariot. He elected him from the seventy-two disciples.

Judas preached about Jesus and healed the sick. Judas was among the seventy-two whom Jesus sent before him to the cities and the villages, He wanted to visit. Judas used to live with Jesus. He followed Jesus. He learned from Jesus. He walked in the footsteps of Jesus but still, he was not saved and died without Christ.

Many times, we go to church, we read the Bible, we have

fellowship with other believers, we evangelise others but still we do not enter a deep relationship with God. The reason for this is that we do not open our hearts and do not allow the Holy Spirit to change us and make us like Jesus. We teach others, but we do not learn by ourselves.

Jesus said about the Sadducees and Pharisees, do what they say to you but do not do what they do. Most of the time, we want to see other's lives changed, but we don't change ourselves and don't produce the fruit of the Holy Spirit.

Whatever Judas Iscariot learned from Jesus, he didn't follow that which is why the gospels do not remember him with good words.

Now he has become a symbol of deception and cheats.

Matthew 10:4 says,
"Judas Iscariot, who betrayed Him."

Mark 3:19 says,
"Judas Iscariot, who betrayed Him."

Luke 6:16 says,
"Judas Iscariot, who became a traitor."

Acts 1:16 says,
"Concerning Judas, who served as a guide for those who arrested Jesus."

Synoptic gospels do not talk much about him but only in the last days of the life of Jesus. But the gospel, according to

John, mentions Judas very soon.

Jesus said, *"I am the living bread that came down from heaven. If anyone eats of this bread, he will live forever. This bread is my flesh, which I will give for the life of the world."* (John 6:51)

"From this time, many of his disciples turned back and no longer followed him. "You do not want to leave too, do you?" Jesus asked the Twelve. Simon Peter answered him, "Lord, to whom we shall go? You have the words of eternal life. We have come to believe and to know that you are the Holy One of God." Then Jesus replied, "Have I not chosen you, the Twelve? Yet one of you is a devil!" (He meant Judas, the son of Simon Iscariot, who, though one of the Twelve, was later to betray him.) (John 6:66-71)

JUDAS ISCARIOT WAS A CARNAL MAN

Judas' heart was after the worldly possessions. He had more love for the world than Jesus.

When Mary of Bethany took about a pint of pure nard (an expensive perfume) and poured on Jesus, it was a significant loss for Judas Iscariot. He said, *"Why were not this perfume sold and the money given to the poor? It was worth a year's wages."* He didn't say this because he cared about the poor but because he was a thief; as keeper of the money bag, he used to help himself to what was given into it." (John 12:5-6)

His heart was filled with the things of this world.

JUDAS ISCARIOT WAS A DOUBLE-MINDED MAN

He was living an ordinary double life. He wanted to live both with Jesus and the world. He always loved the world more and the things of the world that is why he sold Jesus for thirty silver coins. (Matthew 26:15)

Thirty silver coins was not a very big amount. It was equal to one-month wages of a village man. With this money, he could enjoy only for thirty days.

Judas Iscariot devalued the eternal life which Jesus could give him. He prioritized the thirty days of life over the eternal life which was available to him. In the eyes of Judas Iscariot, the value of the life of Jesus Christ was less than thirty silver coins.

JUDAS ISCARIOT GOT ETERNAL DEATH

Scripture tells us that in the end, he committed suicide. Bible says that the devil entered Judas.

The devil always speaks lies. Satan promises to give us a blanket but instead gives us sack clothes. Satan promises to provide freedom and independence but instead bind us into the eternal chains. He promises to give linens but instead gives us rags. He promises to provide refreshing water but instead provides us with cup full of poison.

Let me share a story with you.

Once upon a time, there was a poor beggar, who used to pray to God every day for money. I want to become the richest. He prayed for several months, but God did not reply to him. He was very discouraged and disappointed.

One day he said to himself that I have been praying to God every day, but He is not answering me. So let me pray to the devil.

DISCERNING SPIRITS

The next day, he went to his room and prayed to the devil. While he was praying to the devil, the devil appeared and said to the beggar, "What do you want me to do for you?"

The beggar replied to the devil, "I want money. I want to be a rich man." The devil said to the beggar, "Do you want anything else?" The beggar replied, "No, I want only money."

The devil said to the beggar that it is an effortless task for him.

The devil suggested to the beggar that next morning, he will become a white horse and the beggar can ride on him in front king's palace. When the king sees this beautiful white horse, he will buy this horse from you and then you will get money. In this way, you will get money and will become a rich man.

The beggar was very happy with this suggestion.

The next day early in the morning, the devil became a beautiful white horse, and the beggar rode the horse in front of the palace. When the king saw that beautiful white horse, he said to himself that this horse should belong to him.

So the king bought the horse from the beggar and the beggar got a lot of money and in this way, he became a rich man.

The king was pleased that he bought a gorgeous white horse with a small amount. In his excitement, he couldn't sleep.

So, at night-time, he went to see his beautiful white horse. When he went to the barn, he saw that his beautiful white horse had turned into a weak donkey.

This made the king angry and said to himself that the

beggar had cheated the king.

The king sent his soldiers to arrest the beggar because he had cheated the king.

So the soldiers arrested the beggar and the king ordered to kill the beggar.

While the soldiers were about to kill the beggar, the beggar asked the soldiers that he wanted to pray for the last time.

The soldiers allowed the beggar to pray.

The beggar prayed and said to the devil to come and help him and save him from the mouth of death.

Devil came and said to the beggar, "Taking you to the mouth of death is my job but saving and protecting you is God's job."

Devil plans to take us to the mouth of death as scriptures say that the devil comes to steal, kill, and destroy. (John 10:10)

MISUNDERSTANDINGS ABOUT JUDAS ISCARIOT

Many people conclude that Judas Iscariot was not sincere and faithful at all ever since the beginning. If we say that it is true, then it will not be fair with Judas and it will be against the teachings of Jesus Christ.

Keep in mind that Judas was a very sincere friend and follower of Jesus but in the last days of the life of Jesus Christ, Judas' mind changed.

According to the gospels Judas Iscariot was a chosen disciple of Jesus.

The other disciples or Jesus did not consider him as their enemy. All the disciples and Jesus trusted and believed him.

In the beginning, Judas Iscariot was a faithful follower and loyal disciple that's why they appointed him as the treasurer. Nobody appoints any person as the treasurer if he is dishonest, thieving, or irresponsible.

Always people elect faithful, reliable, and trustworthy people as their treasurer.

If we say that Jesus chose Judas so that he could betray Him, then it is against the teachings of Jesus Christ. Jesus does not choose people to throw them into the pit of sin.

Jesus chose him because He wanted to allow him to change and follow the truth. Jesus wanted that Judas seeks God to change his heart and take away every kind of bitterness, anger, greed, and stubbornness. Jesus wanted to save his soul. Jesus always showed his love, grace, and mercy to Judas; that is why He had washed his feet. But even that act of love and kindness did not touch his heart.

His heart hardened. He had sold his soul to the devil. The life of Judas is an excellent example for us. Judas started off very well, but his end was tragic. He followed Jesus, but his heart was away from Jesus. He received Christ as his Lord and Saviour, he listened to His teaching, he served Jesus, but his heart and life were not changed.

Judas lived and walked with the water of life, but still, he died thirsty. He had listened to the word of life, but he died an eternal death.

These days, the spirit of Judas, which is the spirit of deception, is working very powerfully in the churches. People go to church, they hear the word of Jesus, they got water baptism in the name of Jesus Christ, they go and preach the gospel as well, but still, their hearts are far away from Jesus. Their lives have not changed. They are deceiving themselves. They think that they will enter into the kingdom of God.

If we are considering that we are righteous and faithful, but we are not, then surely we will die and will be short of the glory of God.

We need to make sure that the spirit of Judas Iscariot is not working in us.

Examine yourself and don't be deceived.

THE FUNCTION OF THE SPIRIT OF DECEPTION

The spirit of deception, the spirit of cunning and the spirit of lying are very similar and they work very closely with each other.

The spirit of deception works in hand with the spirit of intellectualism.

The spirit of deception expects praise and worship from people. It always believes that he is a great person.

The spirit of deception mostly works with the spirit of lying. A person with a lying spirit cannot speak the truth. The words they speak may appear to be accurate, but the root of the deception is false impressions.

The spirit of deception takes rulership over the body, soul, and spirit. Then you obey the voice and the will of this spirit.

PRAYER

I bind and renounce the spirit of deception from my life right now in Jesus' name.

Dear God in Heaven, I will not accept the lies of the

enemy against my soul, against my own life and my better judgment. I reject all forms of deception that Satan has tried to sow into my own heart from childhood to this point in my life.

I come against every lie that tried to find a home in my life, in my mind, in my heart and my soul. I reject it in Jesus' name. I receive the truth of what the Word of God declares me to be. I am a child of God.

I am fearfully and wonderfully made. I am loved by God, called by God, chosen by God, anointed by God, and appointed by God for such a time as this. My life counts—my life matters. I have a purpose.

I have a future and I have a destiny that I must fulfil through the grace of the Lord Jesus Christ and the power of the Holy Spirit. I will remain faithful to the word of God and the teachings of scripture.

In Jesus' mighty name, I pray.

Amen.

CHAPTER 10
THE SPIRIT OF TRUE HAPPINESS AND JOY (NOAH)

HOW I MET MY WIFE

When I was working with Pakistan Campus Crusade for Christ in June 2002, we had a students conference in Rawalpindi. I was the MC (Master of Ceremonies), and my future wife was also present there to give a talk. When I invited her to the stage for the speech, I mispronounced her name. When she came on the stage in front of 500 students, she told me off for the mispronunciation and I felt very embarrassed. After her talk, I did not show my face to her during the whole conference.

A week later, I was coming back from the cell group and God spoke to me and said what about that girl who told me off at the conference. I said, "No Lord, I will not marry her and if I marry, I am sure she would be telling me off the whole of my life." But this thought became heavier and heavier on my heart and mind. Then I decided to go to a

Retreat Centre for ten days for prayer and fasting because I wanted to make sure that this is God who is leading me toward this girl.

On the 8th day in the retreat centre, God spoke to me again and said that I have already revealed my will to you. I said to God, "If it is you who is speaking to me, and it is not my thoughts then talk to the leader of this retreat centre and let him come and tell me that my prayer has been answered, and I need to go back." While I was still praying, the leader of the retreat centre came and knocked at my door and told me that he thinks that my prayer has been answered and I need to go back. I thanked the Lord and packed my bag and went home.

After some days, I was doubtful again and woke up at 2am and prayed and asked God to confirm it also to me. So, I planned to cast lots and wrote the below in five pieces of paper.

1. The right time and right girl.
2. Right time but not right girl.
3. Not the right time but right girl.
4. The not right time and not the right girl.
5. Empty (both are not God's will).

I folded all these papers and shuffled them and prayed to God to show me His will again. I case the lots on the floor and picked up one paper and when I opened it, it was the one which had "right time and right girl." I thanked God and slept.

A few days later, I was confused again and was not sure

what to do. I said to God Father, I do not want to make any mistake. I want 100% assurance. So, I fasted and went to a park and spent the whole day with God and in the evening when I was sitting near the swing, two children came and started playing there. A girl, around 6 to 7 years old, came and asked me what I was doing there. I told her that I was praying because I want to know the will of God for my life, and she quickly replied to me that God had already told me his will. When I came back from the park, all my doubts were gone.

Then I decided that I will not approach this girl but will talk to her pastor and will enquire about her spiritual life and then tell him what I want. I went to speak to her pastor and when I was talking to him, he started crying because he said to me the night before I went to him God woke him up and told him to pray for the marriage of this girl. He told me that I was the answer to his prayer.

He said to me that he will go and will talk to the girl and her family if they accept this proposal, it will be great; otherwise, he will not be able to do anything for me. I agreed with him.

When I was going back to Islamabad on the bus, I talked to God and said to him that if it is your will then let this girl and her family accept this proposal without talking to me. That pastor told me that I could call him after three days. When I called him after three days the pastor said to me that the girl and her family had accepted my proposal. Then within six months, I got married to this girl.

Darkhshinda, my wife, is exactly what I prayed. She is very submissive, supportive, and cooperative. She has never scolded me in the last 17 years, and we are contented. God has blessed us with three beautiful daughters - Naysa, Remelia and Nathania.

I have true love, peace, and joy in my life and for this; I give all the glory to God.

Genesis 6:6-9
"The Lord regretted that he had made human beings on the earth and his heart was distraught. So, the Lord said, "I will wipe from the face of the earth the human race I have created- and with them the animals, the birds and the creatures that move along the ground for I regret that I have made them." But Noah found favour in the eyes of the Lord. It is the account of Noah and his family. Noah was a righteous man, blameless among the people of his time and he walked faithfully with God."

Pleasing God is the primary purpose of our lives on earth.

If pleasing God is the primary purpose of our lives, then the question is, "How can we please God?"

Ephesians 5:10 says that,
"And find out what pleases the Lord."

Bible is full of the life stories of the people who pleased the heart of God. The way God wanted.

Among so many people who pleased the heart of God was Noah. Noah was filled with the spirit of true happiness, joy, and commitment.

In the days of Noah, nobody was following God. They

all fell short from the glory to God. The whole world was fallen apart in sin.

Every person was following his pleasure, not the pleasure of God. They were not living their lives according to the Word of God. They were following their lustful desires.

God searched the whole world, but he could not find any person who wanted to please God except Noah. That is why Bible says that, *"The Lord grieved that He had made man on the earth and His heart filled with pain."* (Genesis 6:6)

But Noah was the man who desperately wanted to please God, that is why the Word of God says about Noah that, *"Noah found favour in the eyes of the Lord."* (Genesis 6:8)

Noah found favour in the eyes of the Lord because the purpose of his life was to please God and follow Him wholeheartedly. He always wanted to do what brings glory to God. That's why God decided that He will kill all the human beings from the surface of the earth except Noah and his family. God chose to have a new beginning with Noah and his family. Because of this new beginning, you and I are alive and living on the earth. We can see five things in the life of Noah, which gave true happiness and Joy to the heart of God.

GOD IS PLEASED WHEN WE LOVE HIM ABOVE ALL OTHER THINGS
Noah showed his love with God above all other things, and he followed God when no-one wants to know God or follow Him.

Bible says that Noah walked with the Lord wholeheartedly. (Genesis 6:9)

This is what God wants to see in each one of us. God is love and he wants to pour out his love into our lives. For receiving his love, we need to connect with his heart and spirit.

If we want to receive his love in our lives, we need to love Him with all our heart, mind, and soul.

Hosea 6:6 says that,
"For I desire mercy, not sacrifice and acknowledgement of God rather than burnt offerings."

We can know the heartbeat of God in this verse. We can understand his heart's desire, what he wants. God wants us that we acknowledge him in all our ways and spend time with him. That is why Jesus said that I give you a new commandment. Let us read it in Matthew 22:37-39,

"Jesus said: 'Love the Lord your God with all your heart and with all your soul and with your entire mind.' And the second is like it: 'Love your neighbour as yourself.'"

GOD IS PLEASED WHEN WE TRUST HIM

The second thing which attracted the heart of God towards Noah is his total trust and wholehearted faith in Him.

Noah pleased God with his total trust and unshakeable faith because he trusted God in the circumstances when nobody wanted to follow and trust God. Noah's faith and trust were terrific that's why Hebrew 11:7 says that, *"by faith Noah when warned about things not yet seen, in holy fear built an ark to save his family. By his faith, he condemned the world and became heir of the righteousness that comes by faith."* Just imagine for a while, one day, God spoke to Noah and said that I am very disappointed because of human beings. My heart grieves because of their sins. Nobody wants to listen and follow my Word. Nobody wants to follow me anymore. But Noah because of your regular walks with me, because of your constant faithfulness and commitment I am well pleased with you. When I look at you, my heart rejoices. God said to him that one day, I would destroy this whole world with water. So that is why you built an ark for the protection of you, your family and the other animals which I will send to you.

Now there were three things which could put doubt in the heart of Noah.

1. Noah had not seen such that much rain in his life which could destroy the whole world.
2. Noah used to live thousands of miles away from the sea. He could say that if he built this ark then how he will be able to take this ark to the sea.
3. How Noah will feed and look after all the animals and his family.

Noah did not doubt about all these things but trusted God for each and everything God had said to him to do. Noah trusted God and believed that whatever God is saying, He will fulfil it as well.

Trusting God means believing God totally and completely without any question. It means trusting His promises because all his promises will be fulfilled.

When we trust and believe God, then He will not let us down. When we trust God, then we know that whatever God will do for us will be the best. He will make all the impossible things possible for us. God will take you to the highest places in this world. He will lift you and will bless you.

Psalm 147:11 says that, *"The Lord delights in those who fear him, who put their hope in his unfailing love."*

When Noah started building the ark people around him used to mock him. I can imagine that Noah's children also faced mocking and disappointment. Many times, his children may be used to face shame because of Noah.

But in all these difficult circumstances, Noah holds on to God. He kept his faithfulness with God. He kept pleasing God from his actions and deeds.

Did you as well face this kind of circumstance in your life anytime when you had to trust God without knowing how the future will look like? Have you believed the promises of God and trusted His Word?

Remember, when we believe the promises and the Word of God, we worship Him.

Hebrews 11:6 says that, *"And without faith, it is impossible to please God because anyone who comes to Him must believe that he exists and that he rewards those who earnestly seek him."*

GOD IS PLEASED WHEN WE TOTALLY AND COMPLETELY OBEY HIM

God gave all details to Noah about the ark, the size of the

ark, the different parts of the ark. Which kind of wood he must use for the construction of the ark. (Genesis 6:13-22)

When we obey God, then it gives us courage and boldness to do things without fear. Obedience is a free will; we decide to do all those things which God asks us to do voluntarily without expectations of the reward.

If God tells you to do something you will ask so many questions. You will think about it for days and then you will consult with so many people about it. But Noah did not do anything like this. He obeyed God without any question.

Many times, as believers, we do not obey God fully. We select some passages or favourite verses from the Bible and follow them, talk about that and most of the time preach about that. We neglect the other passages or commandments of the Bible. Like we say that I will go to church, but I will not pay my tithes. I will read my Bible, but I will not forgive so and so person.

But remember, my friend, half obedience is total disobedience and even one small sin in our lives can lead us to eternal destruction and in chains.

For example, if you want to bake a cake. You add all the right ingredients, but you add just one element which is not appropriate like a spoon of red chilli?

Will you eat this delicious cake?

No. Nobody will eat that cake. In the same way, God wants our total submission and faithfulness.

God does not expect from us to be a hundred per cent perfect or holy, but He does expect us to obey Him a hundred per cent. While we are on this earth, we cannot become a hundred percent perfect or holy, but we can become a hundred percent obedient.

We can't become righteous with our efforts, but we can become righteous by the grace of God.

So remember, you can please God by your obedience and constant walk with Him.

1 Samuel 15:22 says, *"Does the Lord delight in burnt offerings and sacrifices as much as in obeying the voice of the Lord? To obey is better than sacrifice and to heed is better than the fat of rams."*

That's why Jesus as well said in John 14:15 that, *"If you love me, you will obey what I command."*

When we indeed obey God, we give real joy and happiness to God.

GOD IS PLEASED WHEN WE PRAISE AND GIVE THANKS TO HIM

Every person feels good when we praise him or say thanks to him. In the same way, God also delights when we praise Him for the great works He has done for us.

Noah always wanted to delight the heart of God; that's why he used to praise God and gave thanks to God when they came out from the ark.

"Then, Noah built an altar for the Lord and, took some of all the clean animals and clean birds; he sacrificed burnt offerings on it." (Genesis 18:20)

Because of the living sacrifice of our Lord Jesus Christ, we do not need to offer any sacrifice of animal or bird.

Now we offer the sacrifices of praise (Hebrews 13:15) and the sacrifices of thanksgiving (Psalms 116:17).

We praise God for what he is to us. We thank God for what he has done for us.

So let us always delight the heart of God with our praises and thanksgiving.

GOD IS PLEASED WHEN WE USE OUR TALENTS AND ABILITIES FOR THE GLORY OF GOD

When Noah and his family came out of the ark, God blessed them and said: "Be fruitful and increase in number and filled the earth." (Genesis 9:1)

God was saying to them, forget the past, move forward with your life and fulfil the plan of God, you have protected from this flood.

Maybe you will say that God is pleased only when we pray, we read the Word of God, when we go to church or when we participate in Christian activities.

But remember that God delights when we fulfil all our responsibilities in the right manner and do what is right before the eyes of the Lord.

In our lives, whatever we do, it delights the heart of God except for sin. When we do our works faithfully and with real dedication, this glorifies the name of the Lord.

You can please the heart of God while you are washing dishes, doing your laundry, while you are driving your car when you are working on your computer or even when you are in your gym.

God delights in us when we use our abilities and talents for the glory of God, which he has given to us. When we surrender all our skills and talents to God, then He uses it for His glory. Like Noah was a carpenter, God used his talent to build an ark.

My dear friend, I want to highlight this thing before you today that God can use all your abilities and skills for the extension of the kingdom of God.

Let us look into our lives today.

Does God delight when He looks at us? Do our lives please God or not? Am I living the life God wants me to live? Am I pleasing God from my life or making Him grieves?

These days, churches need the spirit of Noah which is the spirit of true happiness and joy because the spirit of anxiety, worry, depression, confusion, fear, sadness, grief, and sorrow are very active.

We need to cry out before the Lord for the anointing of Noah, which can help us to walk with God with total submission. That is the only way; we can please God from our lives.

Let the spirit of Noah work in you completely and totally.

THE FUNCTION OF THE SPIRIT OF HAPPINESS AND JOY

Our established careers, essential titles, wealth, power, possessions, degrees, or our significant achievements in life cannot give us true happiness.

Happiness is a gift of the Holy Spirit. Satisfaction is not what you have, but true happiness comes in your life when you do the things God has called you to do.

Happiness is not a reward for doing things for God. It is a consequence of your intimate relationship with God. The pleasure of your life depends on how close your relationship with God is. The more you live closer to God, the happier you will be in your life.

PRAYER

Father in the name of Jesus Christ, today I choose happiness and joy in my life. I choose to be centred and grounded in you. I am grateful for my life that you have filled with many blessings.

Heavenly Father set me free from all needless anxiety, solicitude and worry. Please help me to desire always that which is pleasing and acceptable to you so that your will may be my will.

Today I humbly submit myself to your will, the Word, and Holy Spirit.

I acknowledge and declare that the only source of true happiness is the Lord Jesus Christ and I submit myself to Him right now.

In Jesus' mighty name, I pray.

Amen.

CHAPTER 11
THE SPIRIT OF WORLDLY DESIRES

MANY TIMES, GOD PROVIDED FUEL FOR MY CAR
Whenever I gave a lift to the people or helped them to move from one place to another or whenever I had dropped leaders back to their homes after the Life Group meeting if there was only one bar of gas in the car on the way back to my house all the four light bars were on. It means that the whole gas tank filled.

Usually, I used to put gas in my car every day but a few years ago in 2011, I drove my car for nine days and God provided gas. Let me share this testimony with you.

On 24th December 2011, I filled gas in my car and every day I was doing all my work in routine and till 3rd January 2012, gas did not run out because I did not have money to put gas in the car, but on 3rd January when God provided me money, first, I went to the gas station. So, when I was going to the gas station around 100 yards before I reached it, my car stopped and then I asked some people from the gas station to push my car and they helped me to take my

THE SPIRIT OF WORLDLY DESIRES (LOT'S WIFE)

car to the gas station and I filled gas. But for nine days the car did not stop anywhere. God provided gas for nine days.

There are so many occasions God provided gas and petrol supernaturally in my car.

Genesis 19:17, 24-26

"As soon as they had brought them out, one of them said, "Flee for your lives! Do not look back and do not stop anywhere in the plain! Flee to the mountains, or you will sweep away!"

Then the Lord rained down burning sulphur on Sodom and Gomorrah—from the Lord out of the heavens. Thus, he overthrew those cities and the entire plain, destroying all those living in the cities—and the vegetation in the land. But Lot's wife looked back, and she became a pillar of salt."

We do not have much information about Lot's wife. We do not know even her name. She was punished by being turned into a pillar of salt after she looked back at Sodom and Gomorrah.

The spirit of Lot's wife is the spirit of worldly desires which is working in the churches very powerfully.

Because of this spirit, many churches and families have been destroyed. In this era, it is essential to know about it and bind it in the name of Jesus Christ and overcome it by the blood of our Lord Jesus Christ.

Let us look at the life of Lot's wife and the spirit which was working in her. Then we will see how this spirit destroyed her life and family.

LOT'S WIFE DESTROYED WHILE SHE HAD THE OPPORTUNITY TO BE SAVED

Lot was a faithful man. He knew God and he used to follow him faithfully. So, we can assume that she knew the God of Lot. She had heard about the God of Lot. She knew the glorious works of the God of Abraham. Maybe she had seen the great and mighty things God had done for Abraham. She may be used to worship God with her husband Lot, or perhaps she used to pray with her husband Lot but still, she died. She became a pillar of salt and in this way; she became a symbol of destruction.

Same way, things are happening in the churches today. People hear the Word of God every Sunday. They worship God. They see God's miracles with their own eyes, but still, they have hardened their hearts. Instead of receiving God's grace and salvation, they are working hard for the things of this world. They filled with the lust of the riches of this world. The door of salvation is wide open for them, but still, they do not want to enter it.

LOT'S WIFE DESTROYED WHILE SHE HAD CLEAR INSTRUCTIONS

Genesis 19:17 says that,
"As soon as they had brought them out, one of them said, "Flee for your lives! Do not look back and do not stop anywhere in the plain! Flee to the mountains, or you will sweep away!"

Then Genesis 19:26 says that,
"But Lot's wife looked back, and she became a pillar of salt."

Angels gave them clear instructions and warned them that

if they do not follow these instructions, then they will be swept away.

Lot's wife had clear instructions, but still, she didn't follow it. She devalued the given instructions. She had no excuse. She could not say that she did not listen, or she did not know it.

She purposefully disobeyed the instructions of the Lord and that is why she had swept away and become the pillar of salt.

Now we have the Word of God in a book and wherever or whenever we want, we can read it and can know the will of God. We can follow the Word of God and can have the grace and salvation which we receive through Christ free of cast. But still many people are unaware of it and going into eternal hell.

LOT'S WIFE DESTROYED WHILE SHE HAD TRIED TO BE SAVED

Lot's wife believed the destruction supposed to come on Sodom and Gomorrah. She tried to escape from this destruction with her husband and daughters. She woke up early in the morning and left Sodom and Gomorrah with her family but still she could not reach her destination. She had swept away on the way and became the pillar of salt.

In these days, the spirit of Lot's wife is working in the churches very powerfully. People know the Word of God. They believe in the Word of God. They take water baptism, but they do not cease the desires of the world. They go after the things of the world.

In this way, they try to please God and the world together. They live a double standard life. They want to follow God and the world at the same time.

The Word of God says about this kind of people in Revelation 3:15-16, *"I know your deeds that you are neither cold nor hot. I wish you were either one or the other! So, because you are lukewarm neither not nor cold, I am about to spit you out of my mouth."*

This kind of people neither follows God completely nor follows the world completely. These kinds of people want to gain both the world and God same time. It is what Lot's wife wanted; that is why she became the pillar of salt.

LOT'S WIFE DESTROYED AS SHE TRIED TO BE OBEDIENT

God commanded her that run for your life, do not look back and do not stop anywhere in the plain. She fled for her life, but she stopped halfway and looked around. Half obedience is equal to the total disobedience.

She disobeyed God. Because of her half obedience, she became disobedient to God and because of this, she got eternal death.

One sin of disobedience can push us into eternal death and eternal destruction. It can separate us from God eternally.

Adam and Eve did the same sin of disobedience. Because of their disobedience, they expelled from the Garden of Eden, which was the place of the presence of God. In this way, God not only expelled them from the Garden of Eden but from his presence as well.

Adam lived nine hundred and thirty years on earth and then he died. (Genesis 5:5)

Adam desired and struggled for nine hundred and thirty years to go back to the garden back to that place from where he kicked out. But he never succeeds to go back to the Garden of Eden, which was the place of the presence of God, and the place of perfect peace and joy.

Sin is sin, whether it is big or small. Sin separates us from God and causes us to go into eternal death.

LOT'S WIFE DESTROYED WHILE SHE WAS AMONG THE SAVED PEOPLE
Lot was a righteous and godly man. Lot's wife knew about her husband's righteous and holy life, but still, she did not follow God wholeheartedly.

The angels of the Lord held hands of Lot, his wife and his two daughters and took them outside of the city. They rescued them from the pandemic, but still, she died.

She was not too far from the city of the refuge. She was very close to the city of refuge and taken away from the city of Sodom and Gomorrah. She was very close to the redemption, but still, she destroyed. Do you know why? Because her heart was bound with the love of the things of this world. Lot's wife could have been saved, rescued, and protected from the pandemic of the city, but still, she was killed.

In the same way, many people have been cleaned by the blood of Jesus Christ, but still, they are dying in their sins. Grace and mercy are available for them, but still, they are not willing to repent of their sins. They are not ready to leave their worldly lifestyle.

2 Peter 2:22
"Of them the proverbs are true: "A dog returns to its vomit and, "A sow that washed goes back to her wallowing in the mud."

Maybe you have experienced too that dog vomits and then whatever he vomits, go back to it, and eat it again. The person who escaped from the corruption of the world by knowing our Lord and Saviour Jesus Christ, He again is entangled in it. The bible says that he is like a dog. As the dog returns to its vomit, in the same way, this kind of person goes back to the things he had left.

Remember! The spirit of Lot's wife is the spirit of worldly desires and is working in this world very powerfully.

These days, we need to identify this spirit in our churches and need to inform the congregation about it.

God has called us to run the race and win it as well. If we give more value to the things of this world, then we will not be able to overcome the desires and the lust of this world. We need to submit our desires and wishes to the Lord. If we do so, then indeed we will enter the rest of God.

THE FUNCTION OF THE SPIRIT OF WORLDLY DESIRES

The bible says that if you love the world and the things of the world, then you cannot be a friend of God. (James 4:4)

Don't you realize that making friends with the evil pleasures of this world make you an enemy of God?

Anyone living that sort of life will not inherit the kingdom of God.

The spirit of worldly desires is associated with three destructive sins: Covetousness, Envy and Jealousy.

Covetousness desires eagerly and obsessively what belongs to another.

Envy is the active resentment of someone because they have what I want but have not got.

THE SPIRIT OF WORLDLY DESIRES (LOT'S WIFE)

Jealousy is the smouldering hatred of someone getting what you believe belongs to you.

The spirit of worldly desires resists you to submit yourselves to God.

The spirit of worldly desires always submits to the devil and his will.

The spirit of worldly desires always keeps you away from God.

The spirit of worldly desires wants you to trust your abilities and skills.

The spirit of worldly desires encourages you to boost your achievements.

The spirit of worldly desires longs for you to become more humanist.

PRAYER

Father, in the name of Jesus Christ, I repent of my ignorance of the love of this world. I ask you to forgive me for the foolish things I have done or desired.

In Jesus' name, I bind every word that has released the devil or drawn his weapons towards me. I bind every hindering force that I have ever given strength to by my words or deeds or by ungodly desires. I break the power of those spiritual forces in Jesus' mighty name.

Father in the name of Jesus Christ, I ask you to guide me in wisdom and understanding through the spiritual methods to set in motion all that is good, pure, perfect, and lovely and of good report. All of the evil and the bad reports, all that the enemy has designed to deceive me, to lead me astray, to destroy me, my home or my finances shall stop with the name of Jesus Christ.

I thank you, Father, that the spirit of God leads me. I have the minds of Christ and the wisdom of God is within me.

Heavenly Father, today I put on the whole armour of God.

I put on the belt of truth. May I stand firm in the reality of Your Word so I will not become a victim of Satan's lies.

I put on the breastplate of righteousness. May it guard my heart against evil so I can remain pure and holy, protected under your blood.

I put on the sandals of peace. May I go out and proclaim the good news of the Gospel that gives the assurance of peace with God.

I take the shield of faith. May I be ready to deflect Satan's darts of doubt, denial, and deceit so I will not be vulnerable to spiritual defeat.

I put on the helmet of salvation. May I keep my mind focused on you so that Satan will not establish a stronghold on my thoughts.

I take the sword of the spirit. May I use your authority over the enemy through your word. I will learn more about praying in the spirit so that I can eradicate any enemy influence over me.

In Jesus' mighty name, I pray.

Amen.

CHAPTER 12
THE SPIRIT OF ABSALOM

CLOUD OF GLORY IN THE CHURCH

Once in the prayer meeting on Friday in the church, we were only five people and one of us said, today we are very few so we can escape prayer and have fellowship. But we decided not to, though we are very few, this is the time of worship, and we will pray. So, we started praying and when we were praying, there was a powerful presence of God, and I do not know the exact time now. Still, half-way through the meeting, there was a very thick cloud on top of the pulpit, it was there for so long and everybody saw it and after a long time, it disappeared. That was a glorious day, and the presence of God was so sweet and all of us did not want to go back to our homes. That was amazing and wonderful, and I cannot write the feelings and emotions we had, but it was glorious and inspiring.

2 Samuel 15:1-6

"In the course of time, Absalom provided himself with a chariot

and horses and with fifty men to run ahead of him. He would get up early and stand by the side of the road leading to the city gate. Whenever anyone came with a complaint to be placed before the king for a decision, Absalom would call out to him, "What town are you from?" He would answer, "Your servant is from one of the tribes of Israel." Then Absalom would say to him, "Look, your claims are valid and proper, but there is no representative of the king to hear you." And Absalom would add, "If only I were appointed judge in the land! Then everyone who has a complaint or case could come to me and I would see that they receive justice."

Also, whenever anyone approached him to bow down before him, Absalom would reach out his hand, take hold of him and kiss him. Absalom behaved in this way toward all the Israelites who came to the king asking for justice and so he stole the hearts of the people of Israel.

Absalom was King David's third son by his wife, Maacah. He was perfect from his head to toe in beauty. Bible tells us that no man in Israel had a more handsome appearance. When he cut his hair once a year-only because it becomes too heavy-it weighs five pounds.

Absalom was not true in his saying, deeds, and actions. Absalom hugged people and kissed them to win their hearts. He showed his love and kindness to the people to show off. He undermined king David and God's authority. He included people in his army for his benefit. He motivated people that they are joining the military for the LORD.

The Absalom spirit is very much at work today and seeks to destroy homes, churches, and relationships.

In these days, many people undermine the authority of the pastor and cause division in the church. They think that they are doing it for the betterment of the church. They create their own space so they can rule over people.

Proverbs 11:3 says that, *"The integrity of the upright guides them, but the unfaithful are destroyed by their duplicity."*

If you are in trouble because of the pastor or church leadership, then you need to keep this thing in mind that this is God who has appointed them in that position. So, God is using them to change your attitude towards them and other believers. God is revealing to you the real condition of your heart and allowing you to change yourself and become like Jesus.

Mr John Paul Jackson writes in his book, 'Unmasking the Jezebel Spirit' on page 129 that, *"When you speak against the anointed servant of God, you sow the seeds of your destruction."*

If any anointed servant of the Lord is wrong, then let God judge him because it is not our job to judge other people.

Let God do his work and let us do our part.

When we start judging other people and leaders, then we cease God to do the work of judgment. In other words, we say to God that you are not considering this well. So that is why you leave it and let us deal with this person or matter. In this way, we dishonour God and challenge His authority.

If the pastor or any other authoritative person has a hot temper or is a controlling person like Saul, then you should produce a submissive and humble heart in you like David.

David had the opportunity to kill Saul, but he did not do so. He allowed God to judge Saul.

When we criticize our pastors or the people who have

authority over us, then we blame God that He did not choose the right person.

Proverbs 21:1 says,
"In the LORD's hand, the king's heart is a stream of water that He channels toward all who please him."

Remember! The pastor's heart is in God's hands. If he walks rightfully with the Lord, he will lift. If he is not walking rightfully with the Lord, then he will bring himself into the judgment room of God. God will judge him, and He will remove him from his position.

When we do not submit ourselves to the higher authorities and murmur against them then actually, we blame God that you have put them there and whatever wrong is going on, God's responsible for that. When we criticize others for getting our benefits, then we lift the devil and help him to succeed in his plans which are sin.

Proverbs 21:4 says that, *"Haughty eyes and a proud heart, the lamp of the wicked, are sin!"*

So let us pray that God protects us from the spirit of Absalom so we will not have haughty eyes and a proud heart. The bible tells us that Absalom was not true in his sayings and deeds. He kissed and hugged people to win their hearts. Let us pray that our hearts do not follow Absalom. We need to say, God everyday search me and know my heart, test me, and know my anxious thoughts. See if there is any offensive way in me and lead me in the way everlasting.

Today, we need to search and know our hearts and examine ourselves whether we are walking righteously with God or not. Ask a question from yourself: Can God change everything? If your answer is yes, then stop criticising your pastor and other believers who have authority over you. Instead of murmuring against him, start praying for him, then definitely, God will change his heart and mind. Pray for him that he lives his life in total submission to God and follows his ways with all his mind, body, and soul. If you are already praying this prayer and nothing is happening, then you need to believe that God wants to bring a change not only in the life of your pastor but in you as well.

Then you need to ask yourself, what is that which God wants me to change.

Let us pray today that we will consider others better than us and we will stand in the gap for the people not with wrong motives but with a sincere and faithful heart. We will not love people to gain their favour or to use them for our benefits. We will be right in our actions, saying and deeds. We will not show our love and compassion to show off. We will not undermine the authority of the people who have power over us. Whatever we will do, we will do it for the glory of God. We will serve others with love and a servant heart. We will bear the burden of those who are weak and will follow the example of Christ in all the days of our lives.

THE FUNCTION OF THE ABSALOM SPIRIT

The Absalom spirit has brought more harm to the earth than

anyone can imagine. This spirit is charming, deceptive, cunning and treacherous.

This spirit brings chaos and confusion to a church or family or any religious institute.

So many decent pastors and loving church leaders have been destroyed by the proposal of Absalom "care" and "concern" for the church and institutes.

The Absalom spirit typically harbours camouflaged bitterness, unresolved offences, disappointments and anger.

The Absalom spirit believes that the authority is not to be trusted, the power is incompetent and I know the right way to handle the problem.

The Absalom spirit harbours hidden contempt, hidden hatred and hidden revenge of authorities.

The Absalom spirit is rebellious and that rebellion will increasingly grow like cancer and at some point, become unquenchable if not dealt with firmly.

The Absalom spirit views himself as competing with the leadership and regularly distorts and misrepresents the decision or directions the leader is giving.

The Absalom spirit possesses a desire to be in authority but not with any pure motives.

The Absalom spirit believes that he is more spiritual or wise than real leaders.

The Absalom spirit is a master in manipulation. This spirit assures people, "you are more special to me", you are my best friend", "I love you more than the pastor loves you" and care for you more than the pastor cares you.

The Absalom spirit seeks opportunities for self-advancement at the expense of others.

THE SPIRIT OF ABSALOM

The Absalom spirit is very critical. This spirit always finds some faults in others.

The Absalom spirit always exhibits false humility.

The Absalom spirit is a thief, stealing the hearts and loyalty of the people away from their real authority.

The Absalom spirit is not only a liar but a religious hypocrite as well.

PRAYER

Father, in the name of Jesus Christ, help me through the power of your Holy Spirit to discern and recognize the Absalom spirit.

I confess and renounce as sin everything I have done under the influence of the Absalom spirit. Forgive me and wash me with the blood of Jesus Christ.

Father cut all my body, spirit and soul ties which have established between me and the Absalom spirit. Cut that linking supernaturally and draw back every part which has been tied in bondage in this relationship. I speak to every demonic power that has taken advantage of that linking, you go in Jesus' mighty name.

I speak to every demonic power of disloyalty, deception, cunning, treacherous, anger, bitterness, disappointment, hidden hatred, hidden revenge, you go in Jesus mighty name.

I speak to the spirit of competition, the spirit of rebellion and the spirit of manipulation to leave my body, spirit and soul and go to that place which Jesus has assigned for you.

Father, in the name of Jesus Christ and by His blood, broke the power of the Absalom spirit.

DISCERNING SPIRITS

Heavenly Father, fill my heart, body, spirit, soul and every part which has been vacated by these spirits with the spirit of trust, faithfulness, love, joy, peace and comfort in Jesus mighty name, I pray.

Amen.

CHAPTER 13
THE SPIRIT OF JEZEBEL

1 Kings 16:29-33
In the thirty-eighth year of Asa king of Judah, Ahab son of Omri became king of Israel and he reigned in Samaria over Israel twenty-two years. Ahab, son of Omri, did more evil in the eyes of the Lord than any of those before him. He not only considered it trivial to commit the sins of Jeroboam son of Nebat, but he also married Jezebel the daughter of Ethbaal king of the Sidonians and began to serve Baal and worship him. He set up an altar for Baal in the temple of Baal that he built in Samaria. Ahab also made an Asherah pole and did more to arouse the anger of the Lord, the God of Israel, than did all the kings of Israel before him.

Revelation 2:20
Nevertheless, I have this against you: You tolerate that woman Jezebel, who calls herself a prophet. By her teaching, she misleads my servants into sexual immorality and the eating of food sacrificed to idols.

We need to know that there is no such thing as a Jezebel Spirit; it is a spirit like Jezebel. The Bible never has the words Jezebel Spirit, but negative connotations and symbolism are surrounding the name, Jezebel.

The demonic influence of this spirit creates rifts in churches, marriages and religious institutes through cunning, deception, seduction, hatred, manipulation, and jealousy.

When people control other people and start using them for their wrong motives, then they control others as much they live under the influence of the Jezebel Spirit.

Most people who are under the influence of the spirit of Jezebel are hurt or oppressed by other people.

The Jezebel Spirit is a wicked spirit that is often associated with females but can manifest in anyone.

WHO WAS JEZEBEL?

Jezebel took the throne with King Ahab during a time of political uncertainty in Israel. She worshipped foreign idols and reintroduced them to Israel (1 Kings 18).

She slaughtered the Lord's prophets (1 Kings 18:4).

She wrongfully killed a man to take possession of his vineyard (1 Kings 21:1-22:53).

She threatened to kill the prophet Elijah (1 Kings 19).

She murdered anyone who protested her introduction of Baal worship into the kingdom of Israel.

Jezebel was a married woman, but she was not submitted to her husband and was not under the control of her husband. When she was married to Ahab, she brought her idols with herself.

THE SPIRIT OF JEZEBEL

Jezebel Spirit never submits to others but always controls others. Jezebel manipulated her husband as well as her children. Her son Ahaziah did evil in the eyes of the Lord and follows the ways of his mother, Jezebel. He served and worshipped Baal and aroused the anger of the Lord, the God of Israel, just as his father and mother had done.

"Ahaziah, son of Ahab, became king of Israel in Samaria in the seventeenth year of Jehoshaphat king of Judah and he reigned over Israel two years. He did evil in the eyes of the Lord because he followed the ways of his father and mother and of Jeroboam son of Nebat, who caused Israel to sin. He served and worshipped Baal and aroused the anger of the Lord, the God of Israel, just as his father had done". (1 Kings 22:51-53)

Jezebel's daughter Athaliah married the king of Judah and as she became the queen of Judah, she followed the ways of her mother and did evil in the eyes of the Lord. She controlled her husband and did what she wanted to do.

"In the twelfth year of Joram son of Ahab king of Israel, Ahaziah son of Jehoram king of Judah began to reign. Ahaziah was twenty-two years old when he became king and he reigned in Jerusalem one year. His mother's name was Athaliah, a granddaughter of Omri king of Israel. He followed the ways of the house of Ahab and did evil in the eyes of the Lord, as the house of Ahab had done, for he related by marriage to Ahab's family". (2 Kings 8:25-27)

HOW TO KNOW THE JEZEBEL SPIRIT

1. Mostly religious people are under the influence of the Jezebel Spirit. They claim that all their prayers have been

answered. They say that they filled with the Holy Spirit and the Spirit of the Lord is working in their lives very powerfully. They show that they are superior to others. They boost their prayer life and religious performances. They give their money to show-off. They always expect honour and praise.

2. The people who are under the influence of the Jezebel Spirit, their family life is disturbed. The women try to control their husbands and children and men try to control their wives. The woman tries to show that she is more spiritual than her husband. Under the influence of this spirit, the woman does not respect her husband. The woman demands that her husband follows her instructions. She proves to her children that she is more intelligent than their father. Under the influence of this spirit, the woman shows in front of people that she is very submissive and obedient to her husband, but in reality, she is not at all.

3. The people who are under the influence of this spirit participate in religious activities very warmly and actively. They do not like to report about the responsibilities which they have given to them. If you help these people, they think that they deserve it. They are not thankful to people.

4. The people who are under the influence of this spirit destroy everything they do or touch. The Jezebel Spirit creates a competitive environment. People become more religious than spiritual.

THE DIFFERENCE BETWEEN THE JEZEBEL SPIRIT AND ABSALOM SPIRIT

There is a difference between the Jezebel Spirit and Absalom Spirit. The Jezebel Spirit rejects authority entirely and goes to destroy it.

The Absalom Spirit undermines authority from within. That is the difference.

The Jezebel Spirit comes from the outside, but the Absalom Spirit sneaks in from home.

THE FUNCTION OF THE JEZEBEL SPIRIT

The Jezebel Spirit wreaks destruction in anyone who winds up in its path.

The Jezebel Spirit secretly tries to rip apart churches, marriages, and relationships from the inside out.

The Jezebel Spirit will most likely not appreciate the criticism. Anyone operating under the Jezebel Spirit likes to be in control of people and is manipulative and will do anything to get what they want.

The Jezebel Spirit always seeks to be the centre of attention.

The Jezebel Spirit attacks and goes after anyone in a leadership position.

The Jezebel Spirit likes to attach to sharp, intelligent and attractive people when it can.

PRAYER

Father in the name of Jesus Christ, I repent of my sins, both known and unknown and submit myself thoroughly to the leadership of Jesus Christ and His Word.

Father, in the name of Jesus Christ, I cut all my body, spirit and soul ties which have been established between the Jezebel Spirit and me. I cut that linking supernaturally and draw back every part which has been wrongfully tied in bondage in this relationship. I speak to every demonic power that has taken advantage of that linking, you go in Jesus' mighty name.

I break the power of deception, seduction, manipulation, control and disrespecting my leaders in my life.

Father, in the name of Jesus Christ, I now declare divorce with the Jezebel Spirit. I declare a cancellation of all worship she ever received through me, my actions, or words.

I speak destruction over the altars, where the Jezebel Spirit received worship in my life.

I break every stronghold in my life where Jezebel Spirit has lived.

Father remove all leaven that has caused me to walk under the control of this spirit, from my habits of thinking, my will, my emotions, and my body.

I pray for restoration in my life and declare freedom, deliverance, healing, joy, and peace in my life.

I clothe myself with God's armour and take up the weapons of my warfare that are not carnal but mighty in the pulling down of strongholds of the enemy.

In Jesus' mighty name, I seal this prayer by the blood of Jesus Christ right now.

Amen.

CHAPTER 14
THE SPIRIT OF PYTHON

Most translations do say Python Spirit, but Young's Literal Bible Translation says.

Let us read Acts 16:16,
"And it came to pass in our going on to prayer, a certain maid, having a spirit of Python, did meet us, who brought much employment to her masters by soothsay."

The Expanded Bible Translation says like this.
"Once, while we were going to the place for prayer, A servant (slave) girl met us she had a Special Spirit (demon of divination/ prediction; Python Spirit) (Python was the serpent god that guarded the Delphic Oracle and provided the ability to predict the future) in her and she earned a lot of money for her owners by telling fortunes." (Acts 16:16)

It is the only passage where the evil spirit has to give a name. The Python Spirit or the Spirit of Python is one of the many terms associated with a particular set of views related to the demonic world.

The Python spirit is referred to in Acts 16:16 where a slave girl who had "a spirit of divination", the Greek term for "Divination" in this verse is Python.

Divination means using witchcraft to try to discover future events or cause future events to be happy by supernatural means. When you see the spirit of divination (Python) operating, you will also see false prophesying and a profit motive. The money will be attached just as it was in Acts 16:16.

We know Python as a mighty snake that constricts and squeezes it prey to death slowly. Just like the snake, the spirit of Python gets around its victims, which can be a person, family, church, or area.

Remember, the serpent in Genesis convinced Eve that God said something that He did not say and twisted the Word of God. The Python spirit is a spirit of fortune-telling. The spirit of Python is different from the Christian prophecy. The Python spirit prophecy is self-induced, but the New Testament prophecy is not self-induced. Paul tells us in 1 Corinthians 12:11 that, *"the gifts of the Spirit, including prophecy, are given as He (the Holy Spirit) wills."*

I am convinced that when we begin to push ourselves into prophesying out of our own heart, apart from the Holy Spirit, we open ourselves to false spirits such as the spirit of Python that possessed this girl in Philippi.

A person who practices palm reading, card reading, use of Ouija boards and other occult practices may pick up demons, or what the Old Testament calls "familiar spirits."

It is important to note that what she said was true. Satan and demons have some knowledge and will reveal their secrets to impress and draw people into their destructive web.

There is no little discernment today that many churches in the modern movement would probably have put this girl on their prophetic team, for what she prophesied was accurate and positive.

Discernment is lacking because the line between right and wrong are being blurred and even erased.

THE FUNCTION OF THE PYTHON SPIRIT

The Python spirit works with the beguiling spirit, seducing spirit, Jezebel spirit, Absalom spirit, controlling spirit and manipulation spirit.

When Python spirit is operating, there will be heaviness, sorrow, depression, and oppression. There will be manipulation involved and people will not be entirely open for correction. Customs and traditions will be vital and will be difficult to tear down. Visions and creativity will choke.

The Python spirit will cause people to become fearful, weak, and weary. People will start questioning their vision, position and calling. This spirit tries to squeeze out of you everything God has called you to do.

The Python spirit twists and coils its way around a victim and suffocates them spiritually. It squeezes the spiritual life out of them by pressing the spiritual breath out of them.

The Python spirit tries to pull you away from Jesus and the leaders God has placed over you. This spirit draws you from one church to another church.

The Python spirit tries to bring spirits of bitterness,

sorrow, and disappointment so that you end up feeling like everything is falling apart.

A Python spirit wants your spiritual breath. In the beginning, God breathed into man the breath of life. Breath speaks of your spiritual life. This spirit squeezes the life out of your dreams.

Remember, the python spirit is a different spirit from the spirit of fear. The spirit of fear makes you feel like you physically cannot breathe like something heavy is sitting on your chest. You know you are attacked when the spirit of fear takes away your physical breath. But a Python spirit takes away your spiritual breath, and you generally do not know you are being attacked by it.

The disciples were going to the place of prayer, but they were interrupted by this spirit. This spirit always interrupts when you are moving into the things of God.

PRAYER

Father, in the name of Jesus Christ I confess my sins to you, and I thank you that your word says that if I confess my sins, you are faithful to forgive me of my sins and to cleanse me from all unrighteousness.

I confess for condoning the Python spirit. I repent for agreeing with it.

Father, in the name of Jesus Christ, cut all my body, spirit and soul ties which have established between me and the Python spirit. Cut that linking supernaturally and draw back every part which has wrongfully tied in bondage in this relationship. I speak to the Python spirit and every demonic power that has taken advantage of that linking, you leave my body, spirit, and soul right now in Jesus' name. I break your hold right now in Jesus' name. I command you to go to the place which Jesus has assigned for you and do not return in the name of Jesus Christ.

Father, I surrender my body, spirit, and soul to you. Holy Spirit fills me and takes me completely and totally for your purposes. Baptise me anew and afresh in your power and love. Please fill me with your fire.

From this day forward, let me never be the same again. Lord Jesus Christ, I acknowledge you as my Lord over my body, spirit, and soul. Please help me to obey you in every moment of my life. Lead me and guide me by the power of your Holy Spirit in Jesus mighty name I pray.

Amen.

CHAPTER 15
THE SPIRIT OF LEVIATHAN

Psalms 74:14
"It was you who crushed the heads of Leviathan and gave it as food to the creatures of the desert." (NIV)

Psalm 104:26
"See the ships sailing along and Leviathan, which you made to play in the sea." (NLT)

Job 3:8
"Let those curse it who curses the day, who are able to wake up the Leviathan." (NIV)

Fifteen verses in the Bible talk about Leviathan and how fierce he is. It described in Psalms, Isaiah, and Job as a being with multiple heads.

When God started asking questions from Job about the Leviathan in Job 41, there was a reason and purpose behind it. God was leaving a clue behind for us to understand something severe and meaningful about Leviathan.

God wanted to reveal to Job that it is not easy to handle a battle with the spirit of Leviathan. These are the questions God asked Job concerning Leviathan. Through these questions, we can know how dangerous this spirit is.

1. Can you catch Leviathan with a fishhook?
2. Can you tie his tongue with a rope?
3. Can you put a string through his nose or a hook his jaw?
4. Will he beg you to let him go free?
5. Will he speak to you with gentle words?
6. Will he agree with you and promise to serve you forever?
7. Will you play with Leviathan as you would play with a bird?
8. Will you put a rope on him so that your girls can play with him?
9. Will fishermen try to buy him from you?
10. Will they cut him into pieces and sell him to the merchants?
11. Can you throw Spears into his skin or head?
12. Do you think you can defeat him?

Here are the answers God gave Job concerning Leviathan:

1. If you ever lay a hand on Leviathan, you will never do it again.
2. You will not be able to defeat it, so forget it.
3. You will not be able to control it; there is no hope.
4. Just looking at him will scare you, so do not try.
5. No one is brave enough to wake him up and make him worry, so do not try it.

The Leviathan spirit is a demon Principality, not just a demon spirit.

The Leviathan's spirit directly challenges the authority of God, and it is a symbol of Israel's enemies, who will be slain by God.

The spirit of Leviathan is against the glory of God. This spirit confuses, distracts, and destroys where the glory of God is embraced.

The Bible speaks of Leviathan as a strong and fierce Marine Spirit that is king over all the children of pride. Leviathan is a spirit of pride, a stubborn demon that speaks in a rough tone.

Leviathan is a very controlling, religious, independent, and rebellious spirit.

When you command the spirit of Leviathan to go, you will usually feel it leave. People often yawn, burp, or cough as the spirit leaves them. Then they immediately feel a shift from their back and the pain goes. They feel more peace and feel like a weight has lifted from them.

Many times in deliverance, this spirit will laugh or mock, sometimes cursing at the one who is ministering.

Some hindrances would stop a person from receiving deliverance from the spirit of Leviathan like unconfessed sin, ungodly soul ties, occultism, fear, unbelief, unforgiveness and rejection.

THE FUNCTION OF THE LEVIATHAN SPIRIT

The spirit of Leviathan will bring you confusion, stress, heaviness, discouragement and separation from God and his people. This spirit brings separation in your families and churches.

This spirit works against the spirit of discernment. Leviathan's spirit expels the spirit of discernment and creates confusion.

The Leviathan spirit makes Christians powerless believers and makes them stressed.

The Leviathan spirit wraps around a person's spine and twists, causing them to feel pain in their backs and necks and tightness.

People under the influence of this spirit fall asleep and cannot stay awake when reading the Bible or listening to the word, or the spirit of Leviathan wants to rob them of learning spiritual truths. It works to hinder spiritual growth.

The Leviathan spirit is the hidden power behind the battle in a culture that seeks to turn people groups against each other by race, gender, political ideology, or religion.

This spirit will lead you to self-exaltation, naughtiness, arrogance, lying, cursing and unteachable. This spirit brings much destruction.

The Leviathan spirit will make you reject healing, deliverance and even the baptism of the Holy Spirit and his gifts.

Leviathan is a controlling spirit that will encourage you to take control of all your circumstances, instead of trusting in God to take care of your situation.

Many modern-day Christians believe the spirit of Leviathan attacks believers by causing them to turn away from God.

PRAYER

Heavenly Father, I come to you today on behalf of my own life but also representing my family, bloodline, and ministry. I know we have sinned before you. I confess and repent of all my sins and behalf of their sins as well.

Father, forgive me for anyways that I have served this spirit either knowingly or unknowingly. Forgive me for any ways in which I have been twisted or have twisted the truth. I have listened to the distortion of the truth or have distorted the truth.

Heavenly Father, cut all my body, spirit and soul ties which have established between me and the Leviathan spirit. Cut that linking supernaturally and drawback every part which has wrongfully tied in bondage in this relationship. I command all tormentors and principalities of bitterness, self-bitterness, jealousy, envy, rejection, fear, doubt, occult, and any other spirits that have been assigned to me or at work in my life, or family. If you are in us, attached to us, or in any way connected to our lives because of the Leviathan spirit you leave me now without causing any damage or harm. You are now under the authority of the resurrected Lord Jesus Christ and His blood.

I command you to leave us right now and go to that place that Jesus has assigned for you and never come back.

When you leave us you will take your entire residue, everything you have down, all that is of your kingdom, any sickness, bacteria, fungus, virus, cancer, death, or infirmity with you. You will take all your oppression, heaviness and influence with you.

Father, I ask you to remove from my life any influence

from the spirit of Leviathan. I reject this spirit entirely and whole-heartedly. Right now, I bind the spirit of Leviathan and paralyze it in Jesus' name.

Father in the name of Jesus Christ, I ask you, please restore everything sevenfold what the enemy has stolen from my family or me. Father in Jesus' name, please repair all damage the enemy has caused our spirits, souls, bodies, or lives in any way.

I devote myself to bring unity, not divided into the church.

Thank you, Father, for healing my heart, my soul (mind, will, emotions) and body. Please clean me, refill me, and reveal your loving words of truth to me.

In Jesus' mighty name, I pray.

Amen.